THE MINIMALIST PHOTOGRAPHER

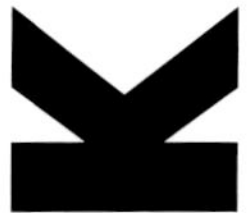

First published in Great Britain in 2025 by Laurence King, an imprint of The Orion Publishing Group Ltd, Carmelite House, 50 Victoria Embankment, London EC4Y 0DZ

An Hachette UK Company

The authorised representative in the EEA is Hachette Ireland, 8 Castlecourt Centre, Castleknock Road, Castleknock, Dublin 15, D15 XTP3 , Republic of Ireland (email: info@hbgi.ie)

10 9 8 7 6 5 4 3 2 1

A CIP catalogue record for this book is available from the British Library.

ISBN (Paperback) 978 1 39962 484 8
ISBN (eBook) 978 1 39962 485 5

Commissioning Editor: Laura Paton
Senior Editor: Katherine Pitt
Art Director: Liam Relph
Designer: Hannah Beatrice Owens
Picture Researcher: Sarah Wells
Senior Production Controller: Sarah Cook

Origination by F1 Colour
Printed by C&C Offset Printing Company Ltd., China

Typeface: Freight Text Pro
Text paper: 157gsm Golden Sun matt art FSC
Case: 5/0 (CMYK + PMS 2202 C) on 350gsm 1/s artboard FSC

Front cover: *Approaching Shadow*, Fan Ho, 1954
Back cover: *Muralla Night Study No.4*, Antony Zacharias, 2022

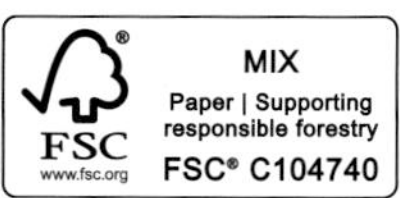

www.laurenceking.com
www.orionbooks.co.uk

THE MINIMALIST PHOTOGRAPHER

50 TECHNIQUES FOR CAPTURING BEAUTY IN SIMPLICITY

ANTONY ZACHARIAS

LAURENCE KING

Composition

Light, Colour and Contrast

Creative Techniques

Storytelling

INTRODUCTION

We live in a world where a proliferation of digital devices, social media and online content contributes to the overwhelming amount of visual information that we face on a daily basis. We are bombarded constantly by an array of images and visual media, all of which vie for our attention. The challenge for photographers in this environment is to create something that is compelling, but not overbearing. We need to make images that establish a deep and profound connection with our audience, and provoke thought and contemplation; photographs that are striking and powerful, and demand the viewer's attention. At first glance, such images may seem compositionally simple and visually straightforward, but on closer inspection they can reveal intricate stories and details that evoke strong emotions.

Minimalist photography is a compelling and widely embraced approach to creating images that can fulfil these responses. At its core, the minimalist aesthetic is about the use of simplicity to distil the visual narrative. Careful consideration of what to include and its placement in a composition can allow the creation of images that are not only beautiful to look at, but visually engaging and purposeful. Simplifying a composition can shift the focus onto key elements, while still telling a complex story. This can engage the viewer by evoking strong feelings of intimacy and inviting contemplation and reflection.

This book explores the core aspects that underpin striking minimalist photographs, with examples from some of the most esteemed photographers. We will start by looking at composition, and see how the arrangement and organization of visual elements within the frame contributes to creating a harmonious and impactful image. This is about what to include and what to omit; how to emphasize what is important and draw deliberate attention to it.

We will then look at how light, colour and contrast are important factors in the overall harmony and balance of a minimalist photograph. They are fundamental in the production of visually compelling and emotionally evocative images, influencing the mood, feeling and ultimately the viewer's visual experience.

Additional creative techniques can be used to direct attention towards specific parts of a composition, while simultaneously providing visual balance and maintaining the beauty of the photograph. As you will see, these are ideas that – with thoughtful use – can help create images that resonate with depth and meaning despite their apparent simplicity.

Finally, we will examine ways in which you can evoke emotion and feeling through your visual storytelling, utilizing a variety of techniques to convey strong or profound narratives that elicit a range of emotional responses. Key among these is mindfulness – a deliberate and conscious engagement with the present moment to appreciate and capture the inherent beauty in your surroundings, whether it's a stunning scene or the simplicity and elegance inherent in the ordinary.

WHAT IS MINIMALISM?

As a guiding philosophy, minimalism places an emphasis on simplicity, clarity, purpose, harmony and elegance. This doesn't relate exclusively to the domain of visual arts and design, but extends into lifestyle choices and, more generally, how we interact with the world.

At its essence, minimalism champions simplicity. It is the 'art of less'. Adopting what can be described as a 'reductionist' approach means that unnecessary elements are removed, while those that remain serve a distinct purpose. This deliberate curation prompts us to think carefully and prioritize, and to include only that which genuinely adds value to a particular scenario or circumstance.

It follows that a minimalist approach promotes a focus on quality over quantity, and by consciously choosing to focus on what is deemed essential, a natural process of mindfulness is applied. Each compositional element is carefully considered for purpose and usefulness, and through this process there is often a deeper appreciation of what is important.

The roots of minimalism go back to Zen philosophy, which values simplicity, emptiness and the essence of natural beauty. Simplicity in Zen is more than an aesthetic choice; it's a reflection of a deeper spiritual reality. Zen teachings emphasize the importance of 'less is more', which is a concept that involves stripping away the non-essential to focus on the essential. However, emptiness is not about the absence of everything; it is about the absence of the unnecessary.

In art and design, minimalism emerged as a movement in the post-war era, as a reaction against the excesses and over-complication of previous styles. It places a focus on the reduction of the nonessential and an emphasis on conveying a concept or emotion with the fewest possible elements or distractions. The intention is to create a unique, intimate bond with the audience, who are invited to engage and connect on a more personal level. Not only are viewers challenged to find meaning and beauty in simplicity, but to incorporate their own experience as they do so.

In lifestyle and personal philosophy, minimalism has gained significant traction in recent years as a countermovement to the consumerism and material overload of modern society. Minimalist living advocates a decluttered, unburdened lifestyle, free from the excesses of unnecessary possessions. This does not mean simply owning fewer items, but focusing on what truly matters. By removing the distractions that overflow in our homes, minds and general daily life, minimalism enables us to focus on the essentials, which inevitably results in a less stressful and more fulfilling existence.

Environmentally, the implications of minimalism are profound, as it promotes a reduction of materialism. This instils not only a sense of responsibility and mindfulness regarding our impact on the environment, but also encourages the reduction of waste and the promotion of sustainable practices, leading to more environmentally responsible considerations and decisions.

Ultimately, minimalism can offer a respite from the effects of overstimulation and information overload. It can be hard to escape the constant barrage of 'noise' that affects all aspects of our lives, and it requires a conscious decision to try to avoid or reduce it. A balance needs to be achieved, along with a recognition that there are helpful, educational and beneficial advantages to the information age, but that these can be accompanied by anxiety, stress and overwhelming negative effects on wellbeing and emotional health. Minimalism is therefore more than a mere aesthetic choice; there are real benefits in reducing the unnecessary, placing focus on the essential and finding elegance and beauty in simplicity.

COMPOSITION

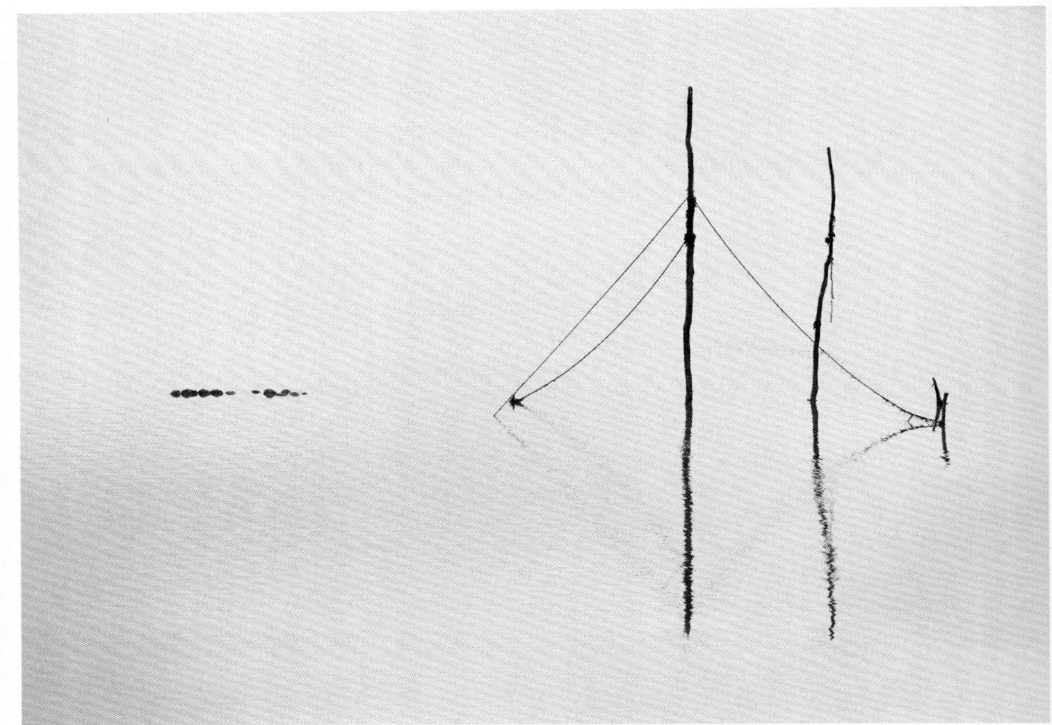

Simplicity, Antony Zacharias, 2019

SIMPLICITY

STREAMLINE YOUR SCENE

A truly minimalist approach to photography is one that embraces simplicity. The removal of any unnecessary and potentially distracting elements from a scene will play a pivotal role in connecting your audience with your subject, and your image as a whole.

This example shows how impactful and visually compelling simplicity can be. The elements are thoughtfully captured against the tranquil backdrop of the water. Although the vertical poles and their reflections attract more attention as they dominate the frame, the stones at the left of the frame provide a grounding effect and help retain a visual balance, offering a soothing and cohesive feel.[1] The colour palette is neutral and muted – almost monochromatic – so nothing in the image confuses the scene. Consequently, the viewer is invited to pause and reflect, and appreciate the quiet strength that is inherent in the elements and the beauty found in simplicity.

When searching for simplicity it is important to slow down the compositional process and think about the message you want to convey. This will help you decide what to include, or conversely what to remove from a composition. What is in the scene that really tells the story? What helps to convey the mood, emotion or other expression you are looking for? Think about what draws your eye and inspired you to create the image in the first place, and pay attention to all the elements in your composition. Ask yourself how they fit into the image and help (or possibly hinder) the main subject and overall scene. The ultimate question is whether each element assists the audience in interpreting your vision and understanding your photograph, or whether it distracts or perhaps even confuses the narrative.

Sometimes, a slight positional change can substantially alter the story or feeling of an image. A few steps in one direction, or perhaps just a twist of your zoom lens can often be enough to reposition certain elements. This can transform what your audience is seeing and have a fundamental impact on how they interpret and feel about your photograph.

Simplicity is a powerful tool that will help your viewer engage with your vision, and streamlining your scene will enhance the impact of the story you are choosing to tell.

[1] *See* Balance and Visual Weight pp. 14–5

BALANCE AND VISUAL WEIGHT

GET THE BALANCE RIGHT

The relationship between the elements in a minimalist composition requires careful consideration. The way they complement one another helps to create a sense of visual stability and harmony, which determines how much impact an image will have.

Balance is a compositional cornerstone that refers to how the elements sit with one another, and where they are placed and arranged within the frame to create an image that is visually pleasing. It is important to consider whether the elements in a photograph work together to bring about a sense of coherence, or detract from the overall feel of the image.

Visual weight refers to the significance of elements in the frame and how much attention they attract. With careful consideration you can use this to guide the viewer through the scene and give them a clear focal point. In this example, the cloud and the rock formations are the key elements in the photograph and naturally draw the viewer's attention. Despite being so different in terms of their physical weight and size, they have a very similar visual presence. This is because larger subjects, high contrast elements and those with more detail and texture (or brighter colours) carry more visual weight. Conversely, elements with less visual weight have more of a secondary or supporting role in an image. These are often smaller parts of a photograph, but they may also have a less pronounced presence due to muted colours or softer contrast.

Splitting the frame almost equally in this example not only helps to give the clouds and rocks equal visual weight, but their positioning also establishes balance within the image. Balance can either unify an image or create a disjointed feel. Here, the central position of the cloud helps to provide equal balance and visual harmony. The simplicity of this scene draws the viewer in, allowing them to pause and reflect.[1]

Once you have identified your main subject, think about where you will place it in the composition. Next, it is key to look at the other smaller elements scattered throughout the frame and to think about whether they help tell the story or just clutter and confuse the scene. Experiment with different camera positions and framing to see how this alters the overall feel of the image.

[1] *See* Simplicity pp. 12–3

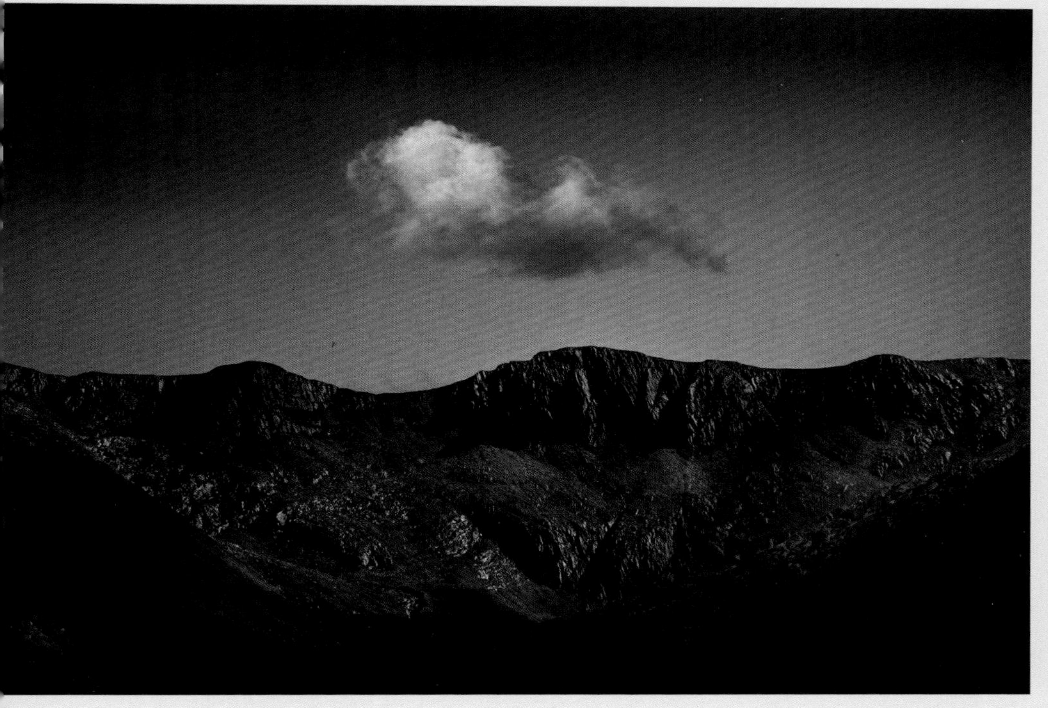

Drifting, Antony Zacharias, 2016

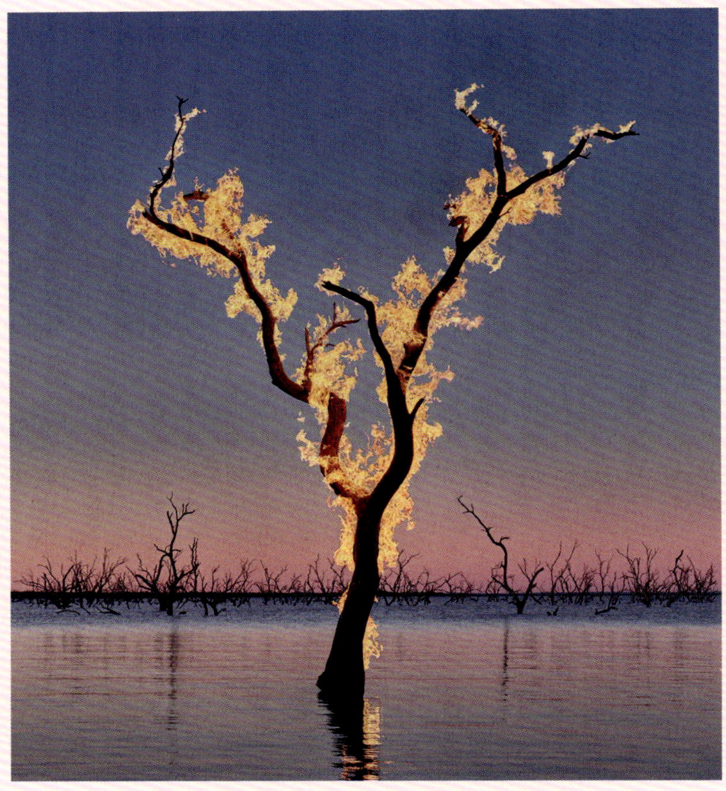

Blaze #17, Lake Pamamaroo, Menindee, Murray Fredericks, 2022

VISUAL IMPACT

MAKE THAT FIRST GLANCE COUNT

The dancing flames engulfing the remains of a tree draw us into Murray Fredericks' powerful image, grabbing our attention and making us want to know more. The urgency of the fire, paired with the serenity of the sunset and surrounding water, creates drama, strong visual impact and an immediate connection with the viewer.

Visual impact is the immediate effect that an image has on a viewer. That first glance – irrespective of the subject or genre – will often be decisive and will usually determine how a visual and emotional connection is made. If the connection is strong, the audience will continue to be drawn into a contemplative journey as they explore the scene further.

Visual impact and minimalist photography are closely linked concepts, and you can use impact to reveal something immediately, with simplicity and clarity. This doesn't automatically mean you need something with great drama or seemingly explosive energy, though – it is often just as effective when the subject is subdued or full of grace and beauty.

Think about what you choose to include in the frame and whether it will resonate with and directly captivate the viewer. Everyone is different and visual interest is subjective, but if an image has a strong initial impact it will inevitably entice an audience to want to investigate further. Impact will not only capture attention, but also draw curiosity as your audience tries to decipher the story or meaning behind your image. As the audience delves deeper, they will create an individual connection with your photograph.

Minimalist images tend to be open to interpretation, which allows viewers to project their own feelings and thoughts onto the photograph. When this dynamic is combined with intense visual impact, the effect is often arresting and deeply personal.

A powerful way to increase visual impact is by isolating an element within the frame.[1] When you combine this with a simplistic composition you will bring the chosen element's significance to the fore, which will attract the viewer's attention and invite them to engage with your photograph in a more direct and immediate way.

[1] *See* Focal Point pp. 28–9

NEGATIVE SPACE

EMBRACE EMPTINESS

Negative space refers to the empty or open areas that surround the subject in an image. In a minimalist photograph, this compositional space plays a crucial role. It is not merely an area that is absent of any content, but a powerful element that helps shape the way we perceive an image. It is a deliberate and integral part of the composition, and the careful arrangement of elements within this space can enhance visual appeal, create balance and direct the flow and narrative of a photograph.

This scene was carefully framed to incorporate and enhance the clean lines and strong geometric forms of the architecture.[1] The expanse of night sky creates an area of empty space, and the graduated light and shadow of an interior window and wall provides a quiet backdrop that emphasizes the visible shapes and structures. This negative space provides an area that helps to accentuate the solitary subject of the composition, invoking a sense of calm and serenity, but also isolation.

You can use negative space in several ways to intensify the impact of an image. For a start, it provides 'breathing room' around a subject, helping it stand out and creating a sense of stability and simplicity. However, this space should not compete with the main subject but complement it. It should provide a neutral area of calm that helps to enhance the scene.

Your aim should be to encourage the viewer to pause and reflect, providing them with a space in which they can engage with the elements and composition as a whole. When you are composing an image, consider positioning the key elements away from any nearby distractions, so as to create a sense of space. Changing your camera position or angle of view can substantially alter how an element appears in relation to others and provide larger areas of negative space in the frame.

Negative space can also play an important role in creating visual balance.[2] The distribution of positive ('full') and negative ('empty') space can be used to evoke a feeling of harmony. It can also be used to establish a sense of depth and perspective by controlling the spatial relationships between the positive elements and the emptiness.[3]

In a minimalist composition, negative space is a great way to direct and guide your viewer through your photograph, naturally drawing attention to your primary subject and the other, ancillary elements.

[1] *See* Geometric Forms pp. 60–1
[2] *See* Balance and Visual Weight pp. 14–5
[3] *See* Depth pp. 32–3

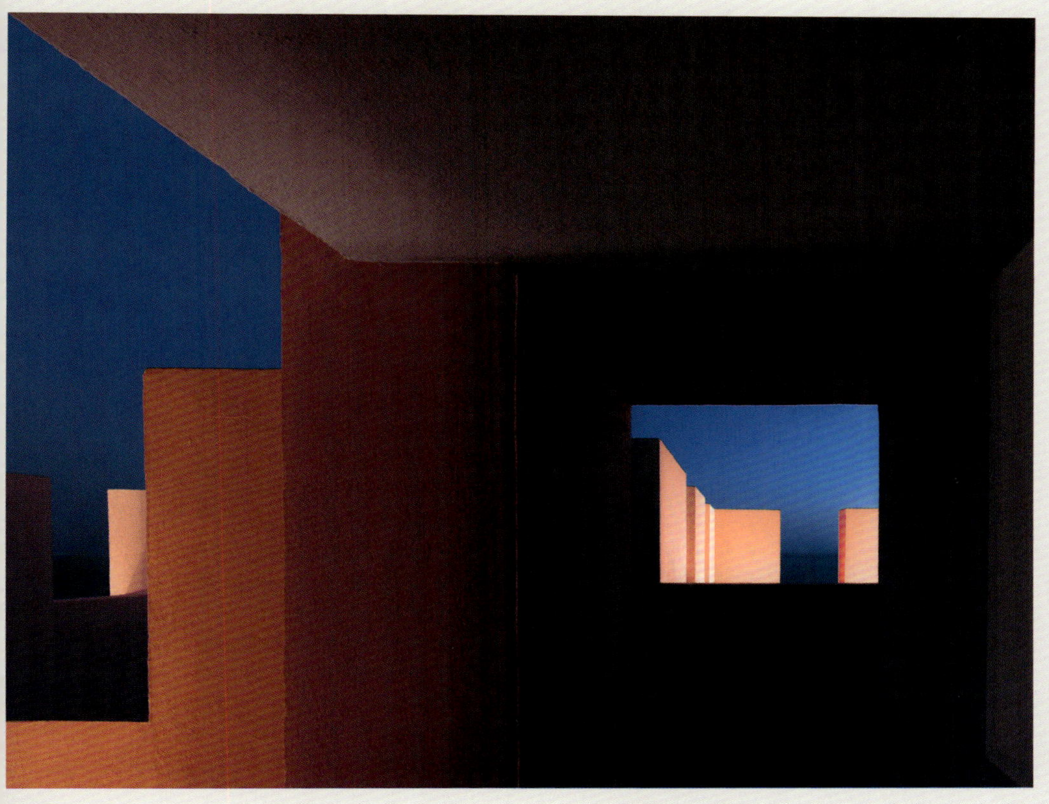

Muralla Night Study No.4, Antony Zacharias, 2022

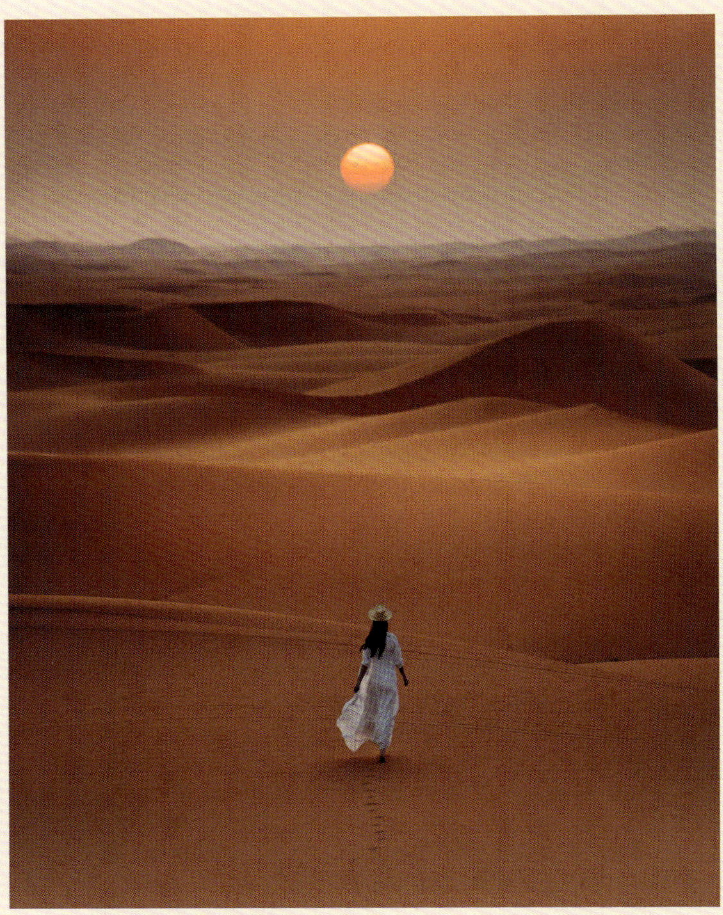

Desert Image, Emilie Hill, 2022

SCALE

USE SIZE TO TELL A STORY

Scale refers to the relative size of the elements included in a composition. Introducing objects of different sizes can be used to striking effect and works as a powerful storytelling tool that significantly influences emotion and engagement with the image. Scale also plays a crucial role in highlighting the beauty in simplicity.[1] In a minimalist photograph, placing emphasis on size and scale can help reveal the elegance of basic shapes and forms,[2] which can transform them into striking focal points.

In this image the inherent beauty of the sunset, the softness of the sand dunes, and the low contrast and monochromatic colour palette all contribute to a wonderful feeling of serenity. However, it is the inclusion of a solitary figure in white that highlights the vastness of the landscape and helps us appreciate the immensity of the scene. While this figure creates a sense of depth and proportion in the photograph, her presence can also be interpreted as a visual metaphor that amplifies the notion of isolation and the vastness of the human experience.

The use of scale in minimalist photography can evoke a wide range of feelings, from mystery[3] to a narrative of contemplation or solitude.[4] The juxtaposition between contrasting elements of differing sizes can often suggest a dynamic tension to an audience; something small placed against a much larger element can evoke a feeling of drama and apprehension.

A strategic use of scale can be used to play with perception and challenge your viewer's assumptions about size and distance in an image. You can achieve this by intentionally distorting the usual size or scale of familiar objects to prompt viewers to question what they are seeing. They will need to use their imagination and curiosity as they seek to interpret and rationalize what they are looking at.

The inclusion of scale is something you can also use to highlight intricate details that may otherwise not be so prominent in the frame. If you position smaller elements against a larger backdrop, for example, you can encourage the audience to pay closer attention to them and explore their subtle characteristics, such as texture, shape, form and pattern.

[1] *See* Simplicity pp. 12–3
[2] *See* Organic Shapes pp. 78–9
[3] *See* Mystery pp. 128–9
[4] *See* Solitude and Isolation pp. 100–03

STILL LIFE

SHOWCASE THE BEAUTY OF EVERYDAY OBJECTS

Still-life photography is about photographing inanimate objects to evoke a mood or feeling, tell a story or highlight their beauty. Minimalist aesthetics overlap with this genre: simplicity often creates a dynamic and compelling still-life image.[1]

The primary consideration is composition, so the thoughtful arrangement of a minimalist still life is key. Ask yourself what message you want your image to convey. How do you want the audience to view the objects in your photograph? Think about how you can create a visually pleasing composition that will still result in a meaningful image – how you choose to tell the story of your objects will inevitably affect how and where you place them in the composition.

The position of objects in a minimalist still life will also affect how the audience views the photograph. For example, you may choose to establish a visual hierarchy based on varying sizes or significance, in which case elevating certain items will convey stature and importance, and even suggest dominance. Views from above will also evoke a feeling of control or power. Playing with the light and shadow can help highlight shape, form, texture and other details, and add a sense of drama to your still-life arrangement.[2]

Reducing your composition to the essential elements will ultimately result in a strong minimalist still life. Negative space can be incredibly influential in the visual impact and feel of the image, as it can often help the viewer to appreciate the subject without distraction, or establish a connection between various elements.[3]

In the image shown here, Harold Ross used a number of techniques to create a visually striking image. Careful control of the lighting has an immediate impact on how we perceive the shapes and textures of the objects, and helps to showcase the beauty of these everyday objects. The intentional simplicity and thoughtful arrangement, together with the use of negative space, encourages the audience to pause, reflect and appreciate the uncluttered scene. While a limited colour palette will often contribute to the simplicity of the composition, here the muted tones are accentuated by the vivid red cloth. This immediately draws attention to the fabric, and in doing so helps create a dynamic, harmonious composition.[4]

[1] *See* Simplicity pp. 12–3
[2] *See* Shadows and Highlights pp. 46–7
[3] *See* Negative Space pp. 18–9
[4] *See* Colour Palette pp. 52–5

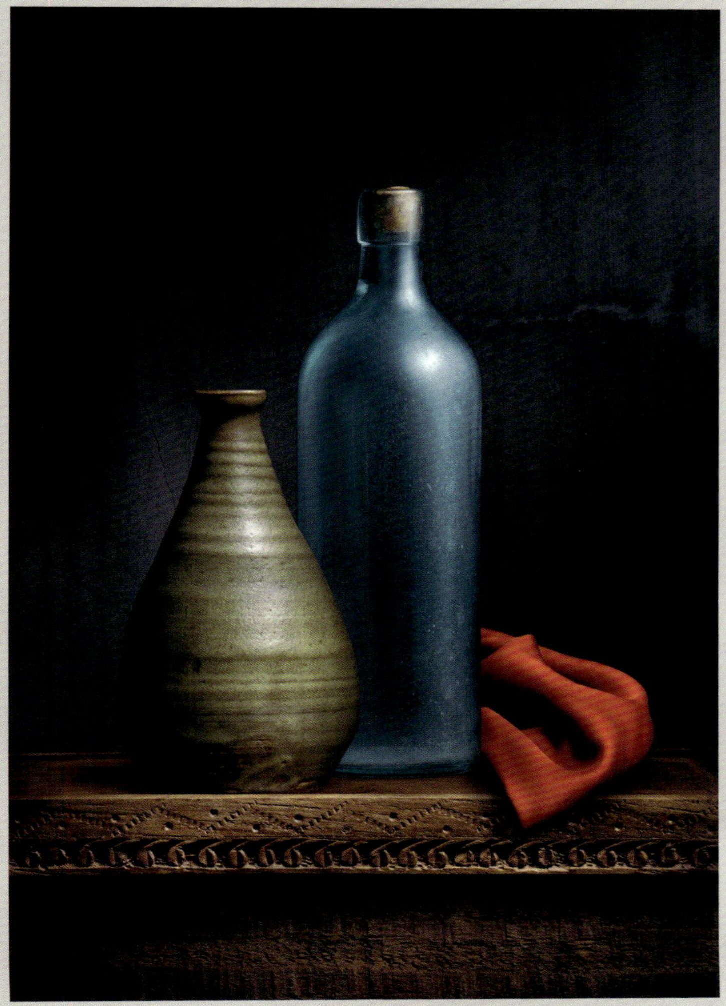

A Simple Study in Red, Green and Blue, Harold Ross Fine Art, 2021

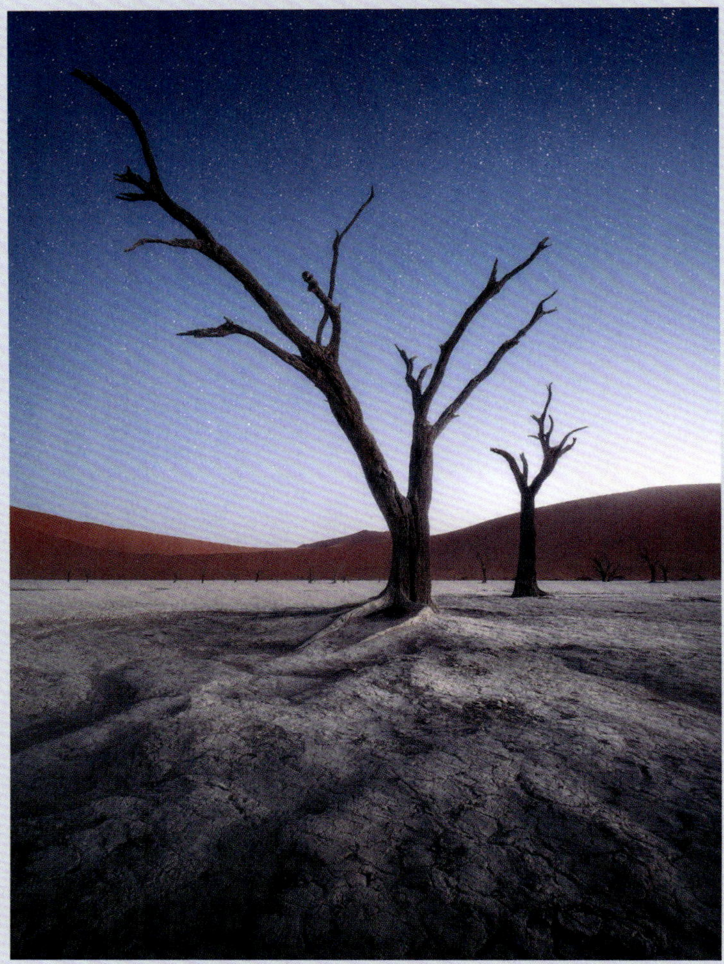

Lonely in the Twilight, Isabella Tabacchi, 2019

PROPORTION AND ALIGNMENT

USE PROPORTION TO CREATE IMPOSING SCENES

In this impactful image, Isabella Tabacchi has deliberately aligned two petrified trees. Each element is carefully positioned to create a sense of balance and serenity. This thoughtful alignment invites the viewer's eyes to move seamlessly through the frame, appreciating the scene as a whole.

Proportion plays an important role here, as the central positioning of the larger tree lends it extra emphasis, adding drama and weight; the other tree seems comparatively smaller and therefore less visually important. Yet together they interact harmoniously within the vast expanse of negative space in the remainder of the frame.

Simplicity is the key here, and the use of proportion and alignment together is a powerful tool for emphasizing elements, guiding the narrative and helping to convey a specific mood or message. Compositionally, proportional relationships and alignment need to be carried out with care; a real sense of intention will render a visually compelling photograph.

Proportion simply refers to the deliberate arrangement and size relationships of the key elements in a composition; how every element differs and the visual importance that each will command in the frame. However, in a minimalist image, proportion is more than the concepts of size and space. A considered approach will help emphasize the relationship between the elements in the scene and create a sense of coherence and unity in an image.

The relationship between the different elements is key. Ask yourself how they relate to each other in terms of size and scale, as this will directly affect the viewer's understanding of the subject. You should also consider the visual weight of each individual element: a small object in a large space may seem insignificant, but the opposite arrangement will suggest the object is imposing and it will dominate the composition and the viewer's attention.[1]

Alignment is how elements are positioned in relation to one another in a scene. It establishes visual order and compositional structure, ultimately guiding how the audience looks at an image. For example, aligning elements along a strong horizontal line towards the focal point can create a sense of stability. Alternatively, you can try a more subtle approach by aligning elements more gradually, so that they radiate from the main subject. Here, the line is more implied and it may take the viewer longer to get there.

[1] *See* Balance and Visual Weight pp. 14–5

PORTRAITS

FOCUS ON SIMPLICITY FOR TIMELESS ELEGANCE

The perfect portrait will capture the essence of its subject, not only conveying the likeness of the model, but revealing some of their character, identity or personality. A minimalist portrait will transform the subject into a powerful focal point, free from the distractions of a busy background or overwhelming details.

In this striking portrait by Horst P. Horst, the essence of the subject has been captured with a timeless quality. The focus on simplicity helps to give a feeling of strength to the portrait. The strong lighting immediately captures the viewer's attention, and also helps to suggest a sense of drama and beauty. This hard light is defined by the long, drawn shadows that have been used compositionally to convey mood, depth and emotion.[1] Hard light is created when the light source is relatively small or positioned far from the subject, and usually produces high contrast with significant differences between the shadows and the brighter highlights.

Finally, there is the angular framing and emphasis on lines that all lead towards the subject. The fabric and contrasting highlights and shadows all help to lead the eye around the composition while adding a sense of vitality to the image.[2]

A minimalist portrait is a narrative condensed into its purest form, where every element in the frame serves a purpose. However, this doesn't mean the portrait has to become sterile or lack feeling. It is vital to think about each element individually and decide whether to include it or omit it; does a particular element add to the overall look and feel of the image or its story?

The considered use of negative space in a minimalist portrait can play a crucial role in helping to emphasize the subject, by creating a sense of isolation and adding balance to the image. Having empty areas around your subject can offer the viewer a visual position to rest and reflect on the overall aesthetic of the image.[3] It is also important to think about where you place your subject in the frame. Will an off-centred composition allow for the effective use of negative space? Will it help settle the mood of the image or detract from it, perhaps creating an unsuitable emotion that doesn't benefit or represent the subject?

[1] *See* Geometric Forms pp. 60–1
[2] *See* Balance and Visual Weight pp. 14–5
[3] *See* Depth pp. 32–3

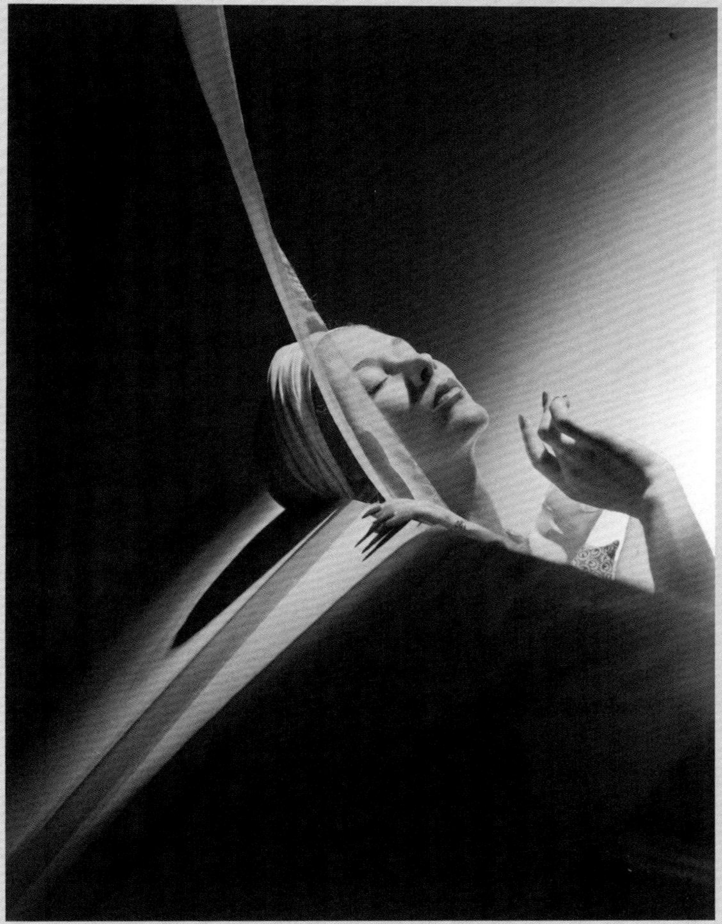

Lisa with a Turban, Horst P. Horst, 1939

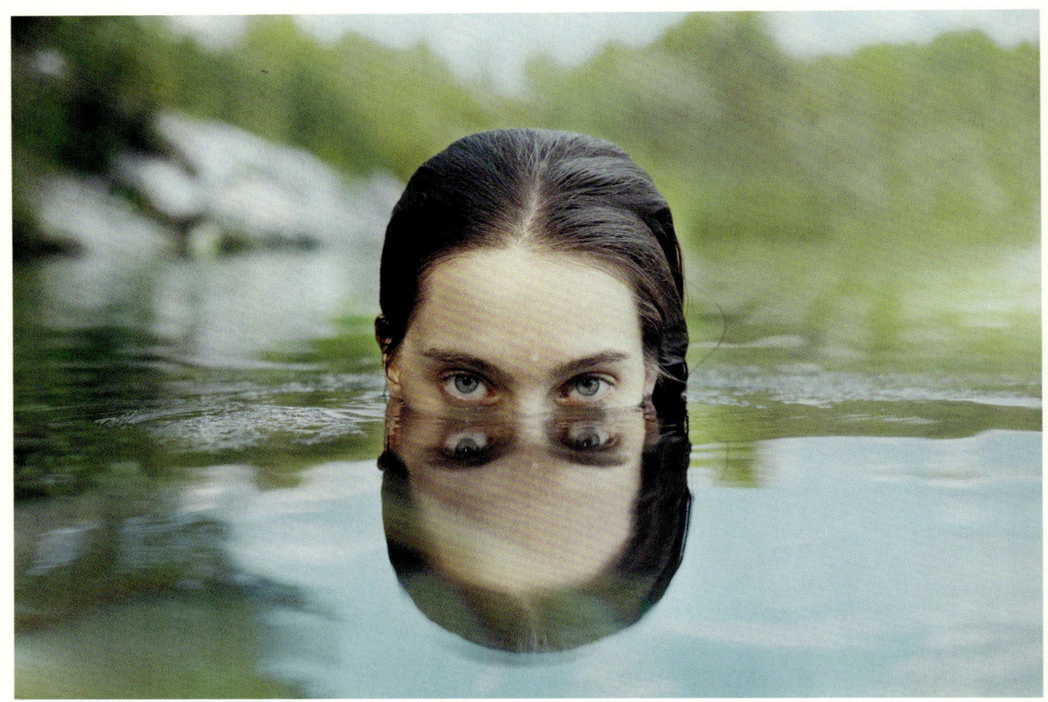

Teresa, Marta Bevacqua, 2023

FOCAL POINT

PLACE FOCUS TO DRAW THE EYE

Marta Bevacqua immediately draws attention to the subject centred in this image. Isolating her from her surroundings and placing such sharp focus on her eyes are obvious visual clues that she and her intense gaze are the main focal points in the photograph. It is from here that we look further into the image – the reflections, location and the fact she is partially submerged – and start to think about other questions.

In a minimal image, it is vital to consider the importance of each element and decide on the hierarchy. Once it is clear what is of paramount importance, think how best you can emphasize its significance in the frame.[1]

Here, the subject's eyes are such a powerful focal point that they create a strong and unavoidable emotional connection. It goes beyond just seizing attention and draws us directly into the scene. It also clarifies part of the visual narrative and invites us to think more about the overall story that we are seeing a small part of.[2]

The focal point is generally the main point of interest in an image; the area where you choose to place visual importance and where you want your viewers to focus their attention. Your choice of focal point is not only determined by the story you want to tell in your image, but also how you chose to convey it. It is vital in a minimalist composition to pay careful attention to all the elements and the clarity and impact of the message should be clear. What you include and choose to exclude is critical. Thoughtful consideration of how everything interacts in the composition will ensure that the focal point serves its purpose effectively and will ultimately control how you guide the viewer through the frame.

Bear in mind that the key focal points aren't the only areas for your viewer to focus on and that the image should work in its entirety. Every element in the frame should help direct the viewer towards the most important areas, while simultaneously providing information or posing questions about the story of the image. Consider using focal points to add depth and dimension, in combination with other elements that create a visual pathway through the composition. Colour, contrast, position and focus – including shallow depth of field to blur the background – can all be highly effective ways of drawing attention to your focal point.

[1] *See* Details pp. 34–5
[2] *See* Narrative in Composition pp. 130–3

FRAMING

BE OPEN TO NEW DIMENSIONS

Compositional framing is a powerful device that can draw attention to specific elements in a minimalist image. It provides structure and balance to a photograph, as the frame becomes a boundary that helps guide the viewer to key elements in the composition. Where simplicity is key, framing can be an important tool in helping to ensure that your audience understands the significance of what is contained in the photograph.

A photograph has four edges that create a visual boundary. However, with deliberate and considered use of framing in your composition, it is possible to create a secondary border to help emphasize what the viewer sees and how they look at the image. This additional frame can serve as a visual guide to draw the viewer's eye to the focal point and help tell your story. It can also help to control what the audience *doesn't* see, which will inevitably play an important role in the visual narrative of the photograph. This 'frame within a frame' is a powerful technique that can deliver a more immersive experience for the viewer.

In the image shown here, Saul Leiter has masterfully used framing to add depth and complexity to the way we interpret the unfolding story. The visual impact of the vibrant red umbrella immediately attracts attention, but on closer inspection it becomes clear that the image was taken looking through a car window. This framing helps to both isolate the subject and focus the viewer's attention. The frame also enhances the visual experience by adding depth. We are seemingly shown a fleeting moment with a real sense of presence and an almost direct involvement in the unfolding events. It is not just a photograph that documents a moment, but a carefully crafted image that tells an entire story in a poetic, meaningful and distinctive way.

It is important not to underestimate how framing can be used in minimalist photography and how it can open up new dimensions in your images. The careful consideration of perspective, angles and interesting elements to use as a frame can all help to transform an ordinary image into a compelling minimalist composition. It can alter the perception of scale and the relationship between the elements, and direct attention within the composition, resulting in a unique and striking image.[1]

[1] *See* Scale pp. 20–1

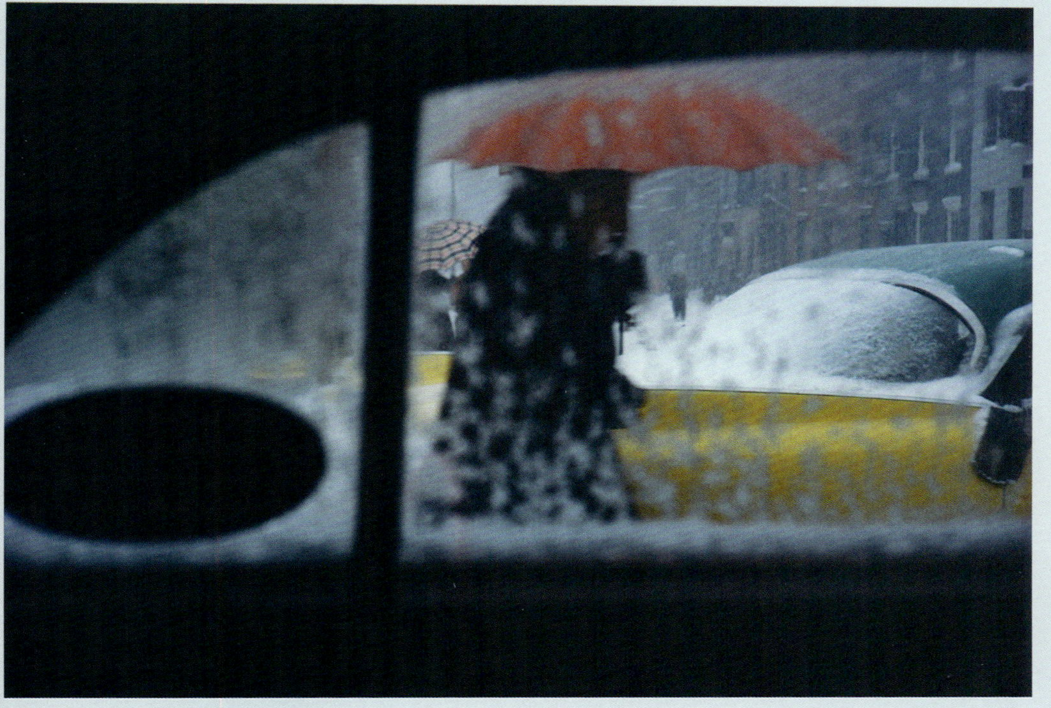

Red Umbrella, Saul Leiter, c.1955

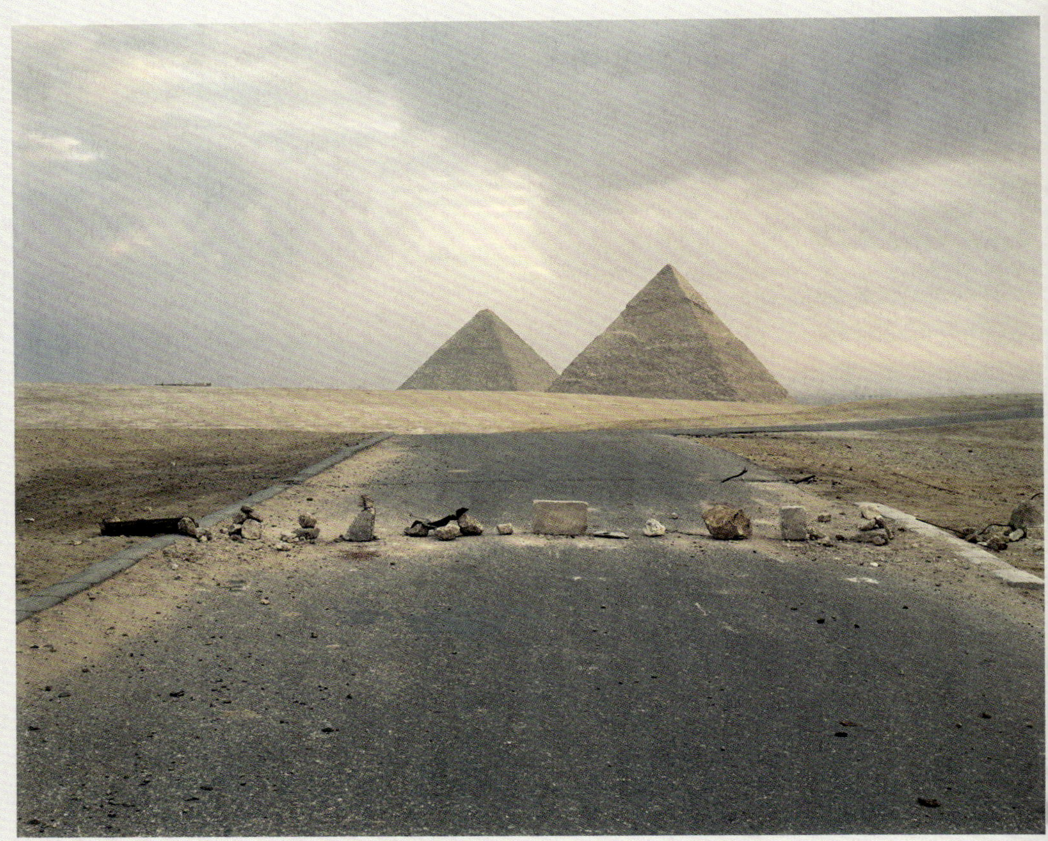

Road Blockade and Pyramids, Richard Misrach, 1989

DEPTH

INCLUDE LAYERS TO ADD COMPLEXITY

Depth refers to the illusion that can be created by extending the perceived distance between the foreground and background of a scene. It transforms a flat image into one with a sense of space, and creating depth can add subtlety and complexity to an otherwise simple composition. It is a powerful technique that can give a straightforward scene a multi-dimensional quality, which invites viewers to look beyond the surface and engage with the photograph on a deeper level.

Depth is not just limited to the suggested physical distances between objects in a scene. It can also help create compositions that are visually dynamic and go beyond a mere two-dimensional representation. The strategic inclusion and placement of elements in the frame, together with focus, perspective and composition, can create an image that reveals a true sense of space and scale.

Layering within a composition helps to add a sense of depth to a photograph by organizing and placing visual elements at different distances from the camera. This is usually done in a way that suggests foreground, middle ground and background, which helps create a visual hierarchy that can guide the viewer through the scene.

In the context of minimalism, layers are not about adding more content, but about adding more meaning. They can bring a subtle complexity that elevates the photograph and makes it more impactful. This intricacy offers a fun way to balance simplicity with intrigue.

In the image opposite, Richard Misrach has included a subtle layer of complexity and visual interest. The road in the foreground leads us directly into the image, heading towards the Pyramids in the distance. As our eyes travel through the frame, they are halted by the literal roadblock midway through. Here, the spatial relationships between the elements become clearer and the true sense of depth is more apparent. This strategic placement of elements on different planes allows for a visual harmony that captivates the viewer's eye, and the careful balance and arrangement between them transforms the image. Rather than filling the frame with unnecessary complication, they work together to amplify impact and suggest a dimensional quality for the viewer to explore.

DETAILS

GIVE CLUES ABOUT WHAT WE CAN'T SEE

It is the detail of the single arm reaching across the window in this composition that creates a sense of mystery and suggests there is much more to this story. It raises so many questions regarding the how, what and why, that it leads us to really think about the scene which is unfolding before our eyes.

There is a clear human connection here, which offers up a subtle, suggestive clue. It is powerful in how it draws us into a more immersive experience as we search the scene for further details, trying to gather more information. This creates a natural engagement with the audience on an emotional and intellectual level and these suggested feelings of intrigue and mystery help establish a meaningful connection between the viewer and the photograph.

The concept of simplicity that is associated with minimalist photography usually involves reducing the visual elements in an image.[1] Accordingly, when composing such a photograph, it may initially seem strange to pay too much attention to the details. However, these details are the integral components that contribute to a minimalist photograph's overall impact and meaning. They are often what attracts the viewer's attention and draws them into the image.

Details can play a crucial role in conveying depth, narrative and feeling, but it is essential to consider what details the image should contain, as there may be limited visual clues elsewhere in a minimalist scene. Ultimately, you should seek out details that will narrate and explain the image and guide the viewer as they explore and consider it further.[2] These are essential for communicating a specific aspect of the subject or setting, contributing to the photograph's overall meaning and adding information, context and direction to the story.

Details can also reveal how elements in the composition are connected and have been arranged with reason and thought by the photographer.[3] This is especially true when your image is more abstract, or focuses only on the essence of the subject, rather than presenting a more obvious or straightforward composition.

[1] *See* Simplicity pp. 12–3
[2] *See* Narrative in Composition pp. 130–3
[3] *See* Context pp. 134–5

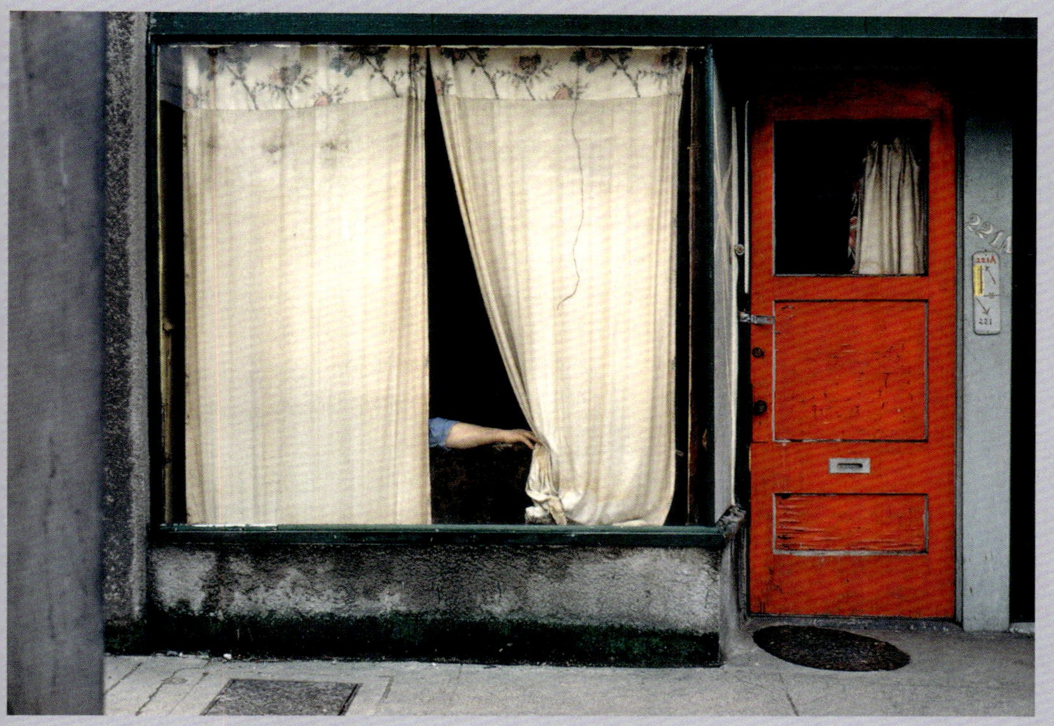

Curtains, Fred Herzog, 1972

LIGHT, COLOUR AND CONTRAST

HIGH KEY

USE OVEREXPOSURE TO REDUCE DISTRACTION

How bright you choose to make your minimalist images will directly affect what your audience focuses on and how they engage with it. However, altering the brightness is not just simply about increasing the exposure; it is about deciding when to use the power of light to alter the feeling of a scene.

A lighter overall image will evoke feelings of positivity and create a sense of happiness, optimism and serenity. Brighter images can have an ethereal, dreamlike quality and those with especially warm tones will be reminiscent of sunshine and sunny days.

High-key lighting is distinguished by its use of bright and even illumination, which helps to create a light, airy feel in images. By intentionally and carefully overexposing the scene, it is possible to remove darker elements, diminish shadows and reduce the overall contrast. This results in a more radiant image that aligns perfectly with the minimalist aesthetic; one that often seeks to evoke a sense of calm, while maintaining elegance.

In this image of an Art Deco theatre, I set out to emphasize the shape of the architecture in a dynamic, yet straightforward way. A high-key exposure has helped contribute to the clean and precise look and feel of the photograph, and has also helped to remove attention from areas of imperfection. This places emphasis on the features of the architecture, which stand out without unnecessary distraction.[1]

Selecting a bright base or background is a great starting point for your high-key images. Adjusting the exposure by using a wider aperture, slower shutter speed or higher ISO – or by increasing the exposure compensation – will help to achieve a bright, high-key look. However, you need to take care when you are using high-key techniques because it is easy to overexpose all of the image. Pay close attention to the highlights and other brighter areas that are important in the composition to ensure that these are not so bright that they detract from the overall quality of the photograph.

When simplifying a composition is your primary goal, placing emphasis on brightness can be an effective way to reduce any distractions: high-key lighting reduces the prominence of minor details. This can be particularly effective when you want to emphasize shapes, lines or patterns, as it directs the viewer's attention to the intended subject, free from any competing elements.

[1] *See* Geometric Forms pp. 60–1

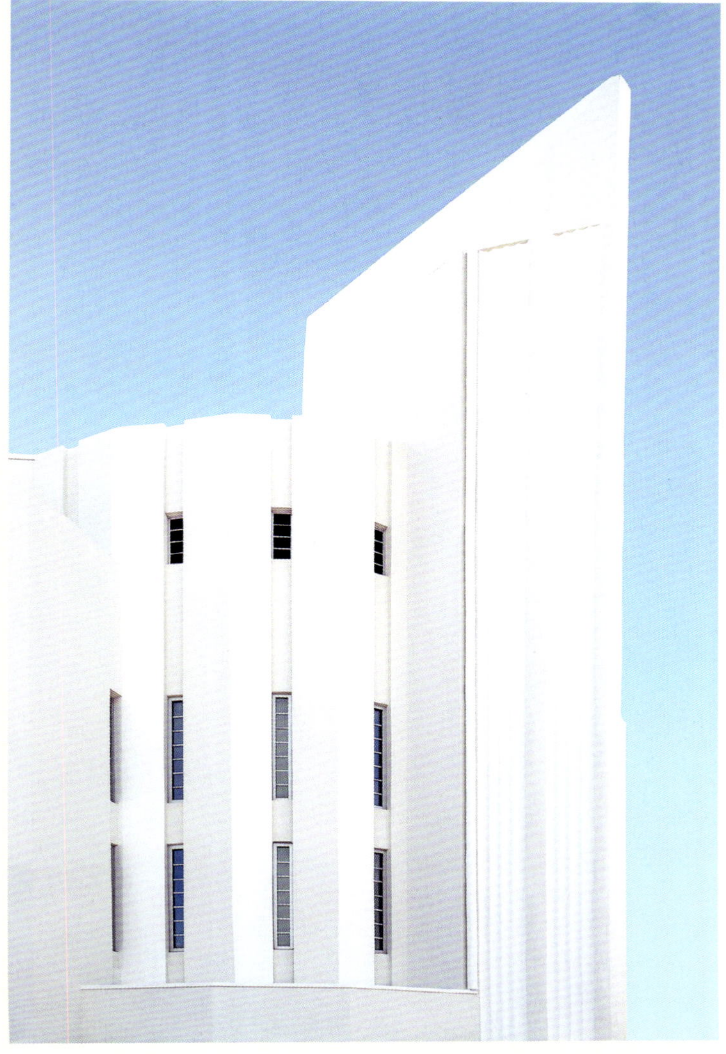

The Theatre, Antony Zacharias, 2017

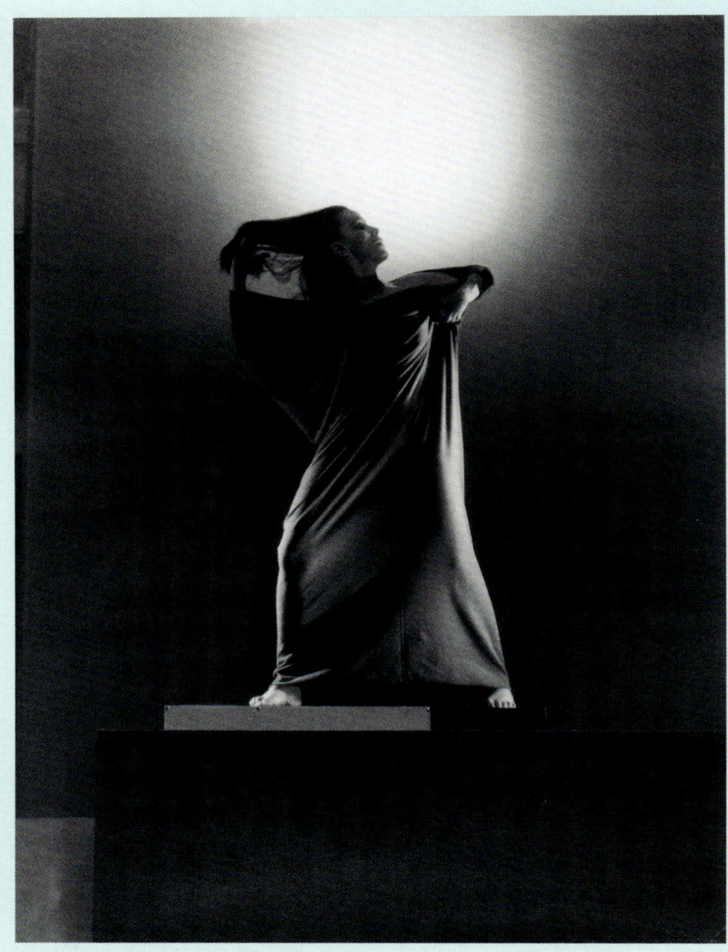

Martha Graham, Edward Steichen, 1931

LOW KEY

CREATE DRAMA WITH LOW LIGHT

Low-key photography places the emphasis on predominantly dark tones to create images that are rich in atmosphere. Utilizing contrast and shadows, it is a technique that draws attention to specific elements in an image through darkness rather than bright light.[1] The interaction between strong light and shadow can create incredibly captivating images.

Minimalism and its inherent need to communicate more with less, resonates deeply with low-key photography. The intentional use of darkness not only helps to emphasize the essential components of a scene but is also effective at hiding the unnecessary. This is not merely for stylistic purposes, though. By obscuring certain details you can invite viewers to actively participate in the storytelling process. Their imagination will be sparked as they try to fill in the gaps left by the shadows, constructing their own interpretations and connections with the photograph.

Here, Edward Steichen's portrait harnesses the intrinsic beauty of darkness and shadows to evoke a sense of mystery and intrigue.[2] By strategically concealing certain details in the shadows, the viewer is invited to contemplate what is being concealed and what is being revealed. This is helped by the fact that the stark contrast between light and shadow becomes even more pronounced around the subject. The contrast between the illuminated areas and deep shadows creates a dynamic tension, infusing the photograph with a cinematic quality and increasing its visual impact. This drama lends a timeless feel to the composition, which was taken in 1931 but remains relevant and poignant today.

Darkness is not simply achieved by removing light. It is an intentional decision to reduce the lighting to draw focus and attention to those key parts that remain visible. When composing your image, think about the narrative and consider which elements should hold more visual weight and importance.[3] Then, you can decide how to use lighting to encourage the viewer to focus on those areas. Start by reducing the exposure, either by stopping down the aperture, increasing the shutter speed, lowering the ISO or reducing exposure compensation. However, take care if you are using a smaller aperture because this will affect the depth of field, as well as reducing the amount of light passing through the lens.

[1] *See* Shadows and Highlights pp. 46–7
[2] *See* Mystery pp. 128–9
[3] *See* Narrative in Composition pp. 130–3

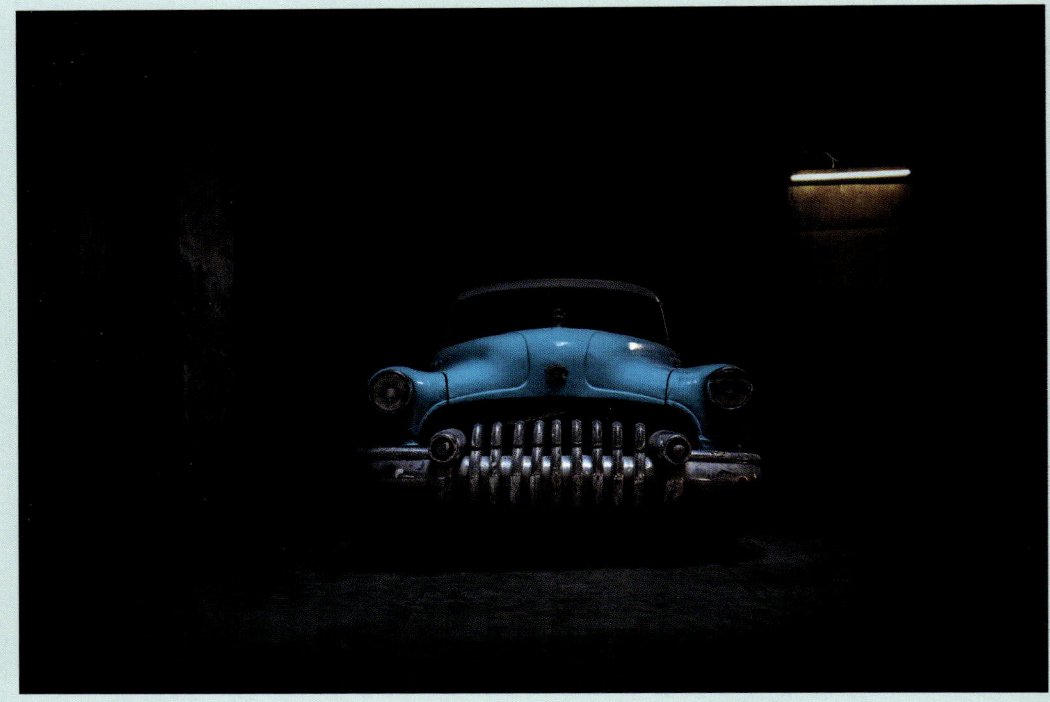

Cuban Classic, Antony Zacharias, 2018

An important consideration when it comes to creating a compelling low key minimalist image is to understand the interaction between light and shadow and how this will dictate the contrast and drama in your photograph. Whether you are using natural or artificial light sources, the direction and intensity of the light is critical in crafting the desired atmosphere. Positioning the light source to cast strategic shadows will enhance the depth and dimensionality of your composition, so think about how different lighting setups can affect the mood and tone of a scene.[4]

In this image of a derelict underground carpark in Havana, Cuba, the selective illumination of the classic car against a dark backdrop allows for a refined and simple visual experience. The fluorescent lamp on the wall provided just enough light to emphasize the overall shape and certain parts of the car, while obscuring those that were not so important. The darker areas reveal little context or detail of the location and so the audience is not distracted by these. This deliberate reduction of the unnecessary ensures that the car attracts the full attention of the viewer, and contributes to a sense of purpose in the image. Everyday objects, such as this car, take on an otherworldly allure when bathed in the subtle glow of a carefully directed light. The additional emphasis from the shadows adds an element of intrigue, prompting viewers to reconsider the familiar and find beauty in the overlooked.

As with all minimalist images, composition is important here, so think about how the elements are situated in the frame, especially when it comes to the position of the light or shadows. Pay careful attention to any negative space around objects and the overall harmony of the image.[5] Frame the scene carefully so you remove anything that is not adding to the narrative, and explore different camera angles and light sources to see how they affect the look and feel of your photograph.

[4] *See* Shadows and Highlights pp. 46–7

[5] *See* Negative Space pp. 18–9

CONTRAST

DEFINE SHAPES WITH TONE

In this image of Skógafoss waterfall in Iceland, I felt that the use of high contrast would help define and accentuate its visual strength. The differences between light and dark create a dramatic effect and a distinct separation between the subject and its surroundings. This immediately directs attention to the ferocity and relentless force of the falls, while still evoking a soft, ethereal feeling. The stark and sombre background is evocative, thanks to the dark shadows and high contrast that subdue otherwise distracting details.

The bright highlights help draw attention to the flowing water, which is captured with a slightly longer shutter speed to emphasize movement. The brightness against the dark background shifts focus to the water and accentuates the movement.[1] The minimalist approach amplifies the scale and isolation of the falls, making them appear more majestic and powerful.

It cannot be overstated how significant contrast is in helping to create captivating minimalist photographs, due to its ability to add impact and simplify a scene. High contrast can be achieved with hard light[2] or strong directional lighting that results in deep shadows and bright highlights, which can be accentuated through careful positioning of the camera. Conversely, soft, indirect or diffused lighting will minimize harsh shadows and result in a low-contrast image.

Contrast in minimalist photography is also a powerful means of communication. You can use it to lead the viewer directly to your subject and ensure that their attention is focused on what you consider to be the most important part of the composition. You can also use it to create a clear focal point, by placing emphasis on a key element, subject or part of the frame.[3]

While high contrast can emphasize drama and intensity through its deep shadows and bright highlights, low-contrast images – where the lightest and darkest parts of the image are less pronounced – offer a softer and more contemplative visual experience. They suggest a more serene and thoughtful atmosphere where the results usually appear more subdued and harmonious, and no single element dominates the scene.[4] The emphasis switches to the shape, form and texture of elements, as well as the cohesion of their placement. Low-contrast images convey a sense of calm, and the viewer is invited to immerse themselves slowly in the subtlety and mood of the composition.[5]

[1] *See* Movement pp. 88–91
[2] *See* Portraits pp. 26–7
[3] *See* Focal Point pp. 28–9
[4] *See* Tranquillity and Mindfulness pp. 116–7
[5] *See* Silence pp. 112–3

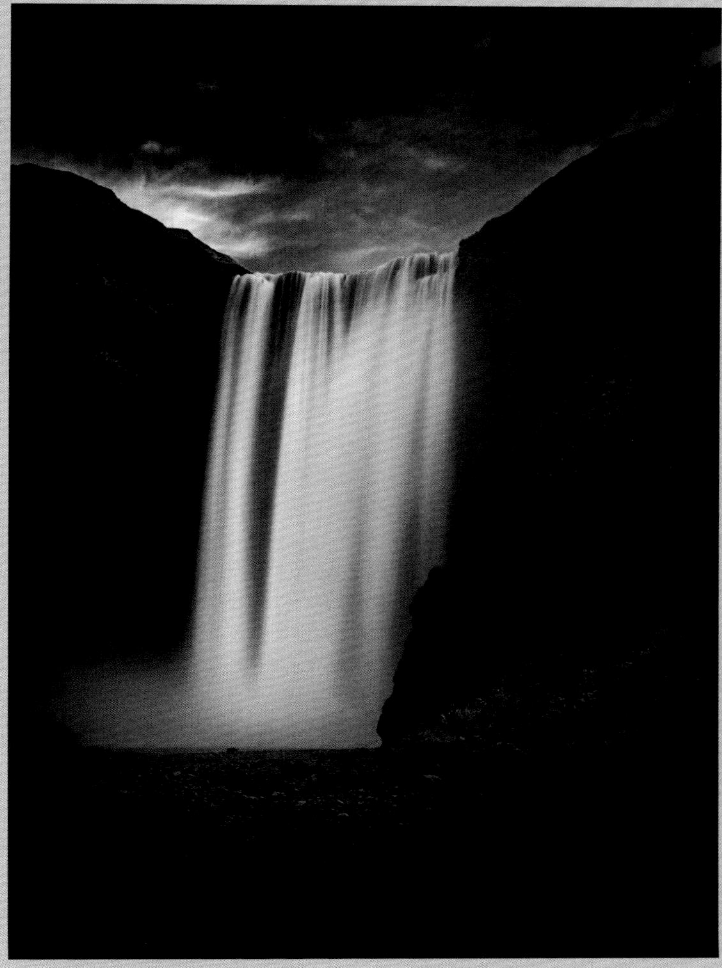

Skógafoss, Antony Zacharias, 2016

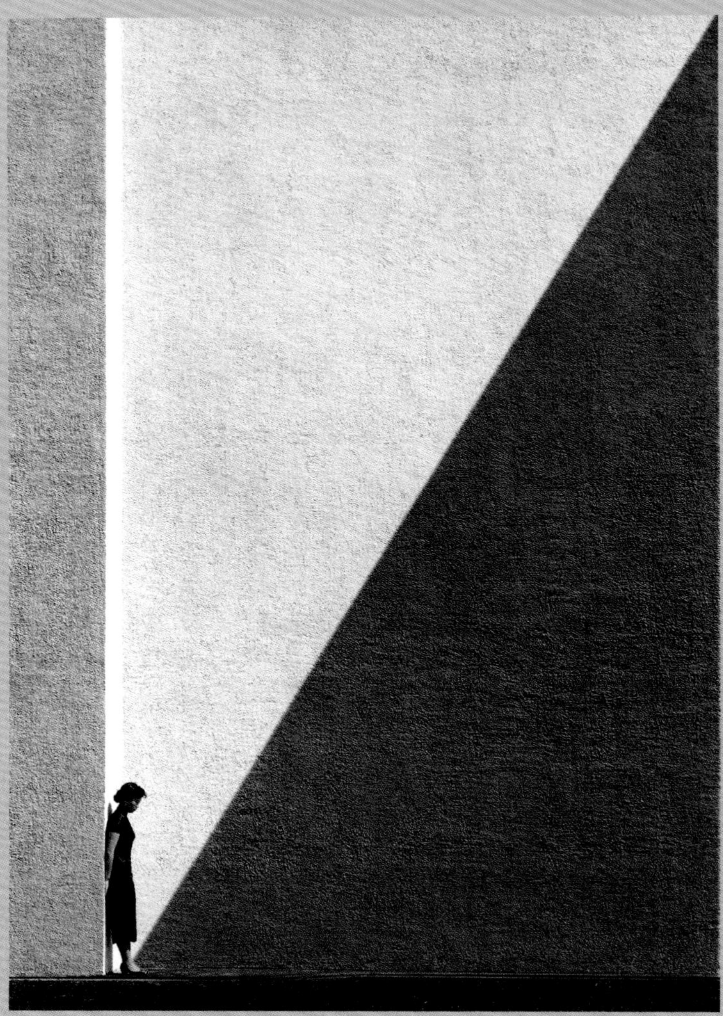

Approaching Shadow, Fan Ho, 1954

SHADOWS AND HIGHLIGHTS

COMPOSE WITH LIGHT AND SHADE

Fan Ho's image, *Approaching Shadow*, is a striking example of how the interplay between light and shade can be used to great effect. The scene itself contains very few elements: the plain wall of a tall building is bisected by a piercing hard line that divides the image into two almost equal sections of light and dark. However, the strong diagonal transforms the static scene into one of motion and energy.

Although the photographer added the line of shadow in the darkroom, it still creates a dramatic visual effect.[1] Despite its simplicity, the image conveys a strong emotional message that is created primarily through the use of light and shadow; at the edge of the imposing shadow there are feelings of loneliness, solitude and introspection, combined with anticipation and contemplation.[2]

Shadows and highlights are fundamental tools for creating depth, contrast and visual interest, and their interaction can be pivotal in creating an engaging composition and uniting objects in the frame.

Highlights illuminate a scene and can reveal and accentuate certain key elements. By choosing what to highlight (and what to leave in the dark) you can create strong narratives within a simple composition. However, it is important to remember that the quality of light will dictate the tone and feel of an image; while harsh sunlight can create captivating and stark contrasts, soft diffused light will suggest a more serene, calmer environment.

Shadows play a slightly more complicated role. They are not just the absence of light, but a powerful tool that can help create depth, accentuate elements and reveal form and texture. Shadows can also be used to decrease visibility and even hide certain parts of the scene, which can reduce a minimalist composition to its core elements.

It is important to think about the balance between the shadows and highlights in your images. Too much shadow may mute a fundamental part of the composition, while extreme highlights can wash out subtle details and quickly flatten an image. It therefore pays to carefully consider the direction and strength of light, and how it falls across your subject or scene. Side lighting, for example, will create elongated, drawn-out shadows, which can help to emphasize depth, while frontal lighting will reduce shadows and flatten an image.

[1] *See* Lines and Pathways pp. 74–7
[2] *See* Solitude pp. 100–03

SILHOUETTE

EMBRACE BACKLIGHTING

A silhouette is a dark, solid outline or shape of a person, object or scene, which is typically placed against a bright contrasting background. Silhouettes are very effective in minimalist photographs, as they reduce a subject to a simple outline that is free from the distractions of colour, texture and detail. This enables the creation of relatively simplistic images that can convey powerful messages through little more than shape and form.[1]

A silhouette provides you with the opportunity to focus on a single subject or a few elements and avoid an overwhelming or chaotic composition. As a silhouette reveals only an outline of the basic shape of an element, any intricate details and expressions are masked, leaving the viewer to interpret the scene and project their own emotions and stories onto it.

Michael Kenna's image is a visually striking silhouette of a rock formation in Japan. He has chosen to simplify the scene, revealing the bare essence of the outline of the peaks in silhouetted form. Their visual impact is increased by placing them against the vivid backdrop of the bright sky and including their reflections in the foreground water. The image is free from distraction and is distilled to its essential elements: three simple layers of water, rock and sky. The sense of drama and desolation is paramount, and the rocks become a metaphoric gateway to what we can't quite see.

Capturing effective silhouettes can be relatively straightforward. They work best when your chosen subject has a distinct shape that is easily recognizable, but interesting dynamic shapes can also create striking silhouetted forms. Ensure you position your subject in front of a bright light source – such as the sun or a bright sky – and expose for the background. This will naturally underexpose your main subject so they appear as a dark shape set against the bright background.

Individual elements (or very few elements) will help keep your frame clean and make it easier for the viewer to 'read' your image; strong geometric shapes, lines, patterns and symmetry can also work incredibly well in silhouetted form.[2] Look to position your silhouetted elements with sufficient negative space around them, not only to draw attention to your subject, but also to help create visual balance.

[1] *See* Organic Shapes pp. 78–9
[2] *See* Geometric Forms pp. 60–1

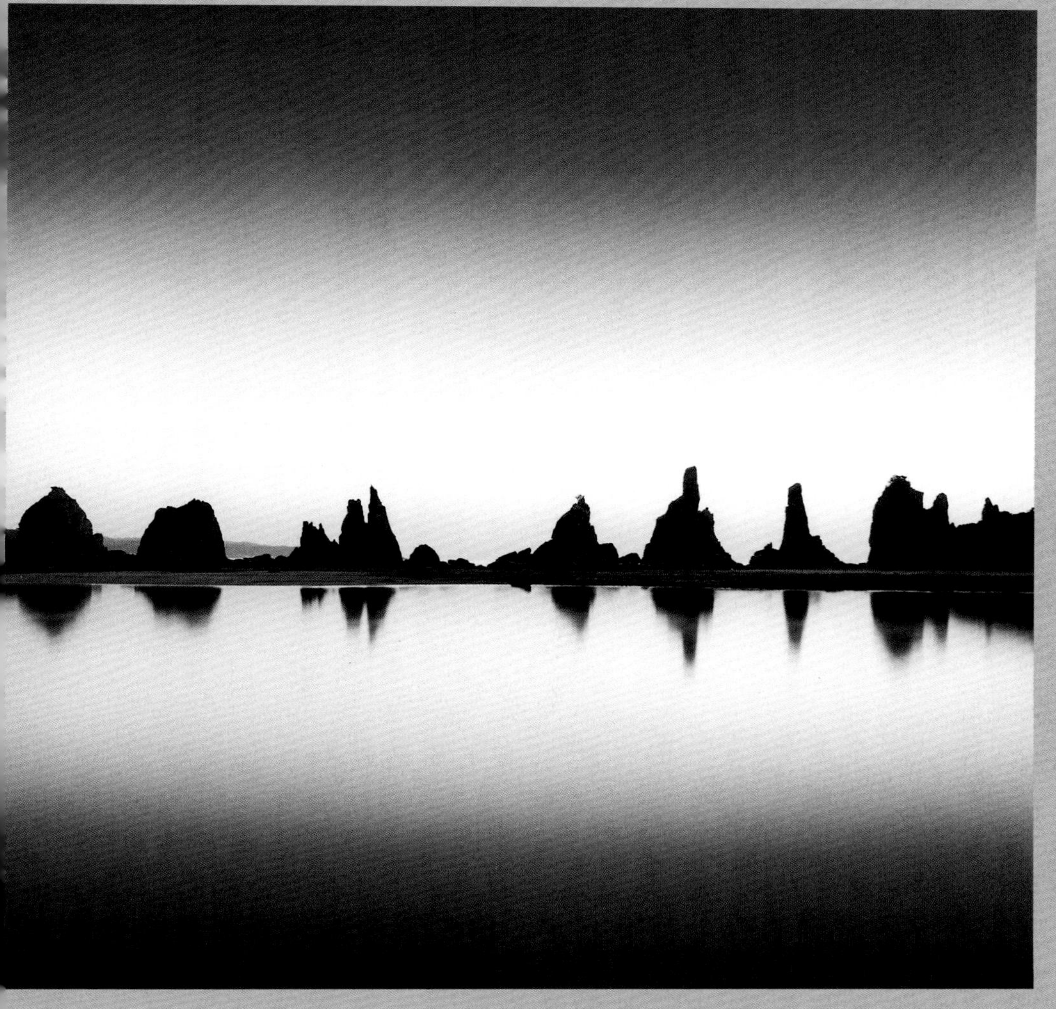

Hashikui Rocks, Study 1, Kushimoto, Honshu, Japan, Michael Kenna, 2002

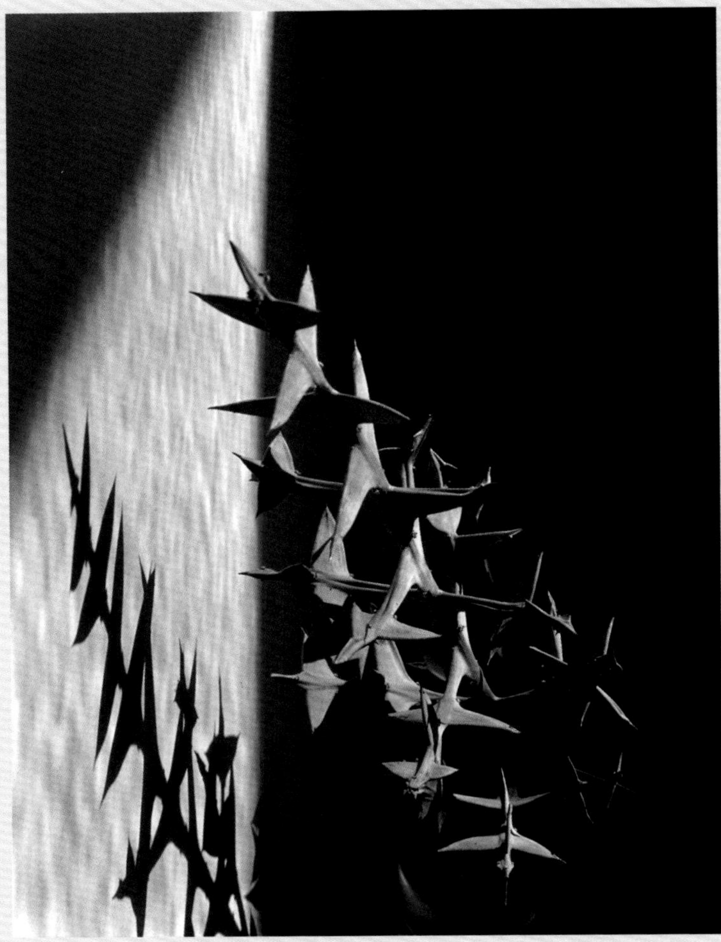

Colletia Cruciata 7, Imogen Cunningham, 1929

MONOCHROME

TRANSFORM THE ORDINARY WITHOUT COLOUR

The visual impact of black and white minimalist photographs can be incredibly powerful. The deliberate removal of colour forces the audience to focus on the core elements of the composition: light, shadow, texture and form. Colour photography can dilute the intensity of these elements, which in a minimalist image will affect how narrative and emotion are conveyed to the audience.[1]

Using black and white in minimalist photography goes beyond just removing colour from a scene. Rather, it's about enhancing and amplifying the essence of the subject. The stark contrast between black and white highlights the graduations of tone and contrast with multiple shades of grey. This contrast can turn a simple composition into a striking image, where every line, shape and texture becomes more pronounced and significant.

In this image, Imogen Cunningham captured the essence of a plant in its purest form, transforming a seemingly ordinary subject into a striking and compelling minimalist photograph. The primary focus is the shape and profile of plant, and the inherent beauty and elegant design of the plant's structure appears more prominent in black and white.[2]

The absence of colour not only helps to portray the plant dramatically, but also emphasizes its sharp and structural nature. The angular composition creates a more abstract feel to the image, which invites contemplation from the audience as they start to see the organic shapes in different ways. There is a pronounced focus on the repetitive form and how this appears almost architectural and artificial in nature.

It is important to remember that monochrome can encompass a range of tones, from the deepest blacks to the brightest whites. A minimalist image with deep, dark tones can convey a sense of mystery or importance, while one with brighter tones might feel more delicate and ethereal.

It can, however, be difficult to picture how an image will look in tones when we are used to seeing in colour. Most digital cameras offer a monochrome shooting mode or the ability to preview images in black and white, which can immediately show how the scene will look without colour. This can be a valuable tool when you're making compositional decisions.

[1] *See* Colour Palette pp. 52–5
[2] *See* Organic Shapes pp. 78–9

COLOUR PALETTE

CAPTURE ATTENTION WITH COLOUR

Scarlett Hooft Graaftland's image immediately draws us into the scene by placing a dramatic emphasis on colour. There is a strong contrast between the warm, intense tones of the colourful pattern that mimics a carpet positioned in the foreground, and the cooler, subdued tones of the surrounding landscape. The vast expanse of the salt flats provides a minimalist backdrop with uniform texture and neutral tones. This is contrary to the vibrant hues of the carpet that accentuate its impact in the composition. The distant mountain adds depth and dimension to the scene, while the blue sky provides a complementary backdrop that enhances the overall colour palette. The juxtaposition between the visually striking colours against the neutral salt flats showcases the power of colour in capturing attention, evoking emotion and creating visual interest in the composition.[1]

Colour can play a significant role in minimalist photography, affecting many different aspects of the overall image. Primarily, when you are choosing to strip back a scene and create a simplified, yet comprehensive image, colour can be a strategic tool that can help to create a cohesive and powerful photograph. It is an important way to help convey expression and can significantly transform a composition when it is carefully curated. The mood and feelings evoked by an image can be dynamically influenced by the colour choices made. Muted pastel tones, for example, can embody a feeling of serenity and tranquillity, while brighter colours can suggest something more energetic. Harmonizing colours can create a sense of unity and visual cohesion.

[1] *See* Juxtaposition pp. 118–9

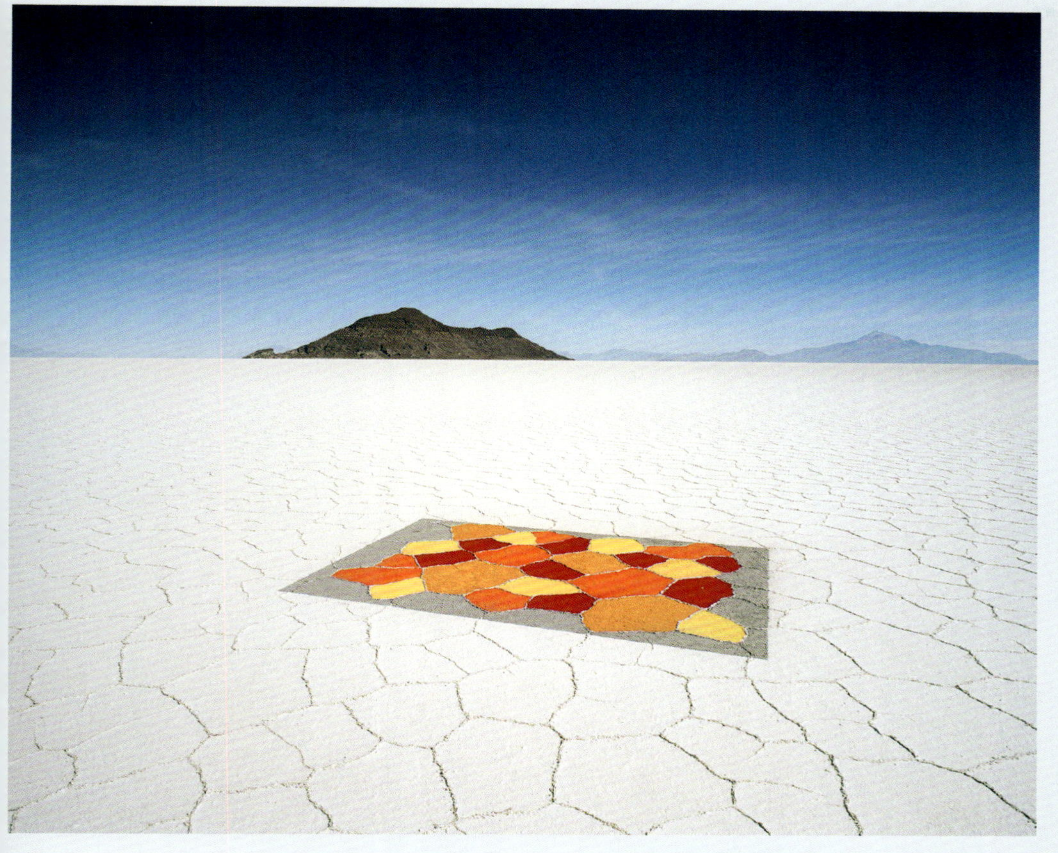

Carpet, Scarlett Hooft Graafland, 2010

Monochromatic minimalist photography doesn't have to be black and white – you can also consider using a monochromatic *colour* palette, where a single colour is utilized in varying tones. In the image opposite by Franco Fontana, for example, the prominent red hues have a powerful visual impact. The consistency of this chosen colour brings a strong sense of uniformity to the photograph; the car and the man in the red hat are still the main subjects and the architecture blends into the frame, despite dominating the composition.

This limited colour palette clearly enhances the minimalist aesthetic, even though there is not a lot of obvious empty or negative space. There is a clear context to the photograph and the emphasis on a consistent colour has created a visually striking composition and helps to remove detail and disarray. It has contributed to making the photograph feel cohesive, and at the same time simple, balanced and dynamic.

Using complementary colours in your minimalist photographs can enhance the visual appeal of an image without the need to overcomplicate the composition. Different colours can evoke distinct emotions, which can significantly affect the mood of a photograph depending on your choice. Warmer tones, such as yellows and oranges, can evoke a sense of warmth and energy, whereas cool greens and blues suggest a sense of serenity and peacefulness. Including these colours simultaneously can help create a robust and pleasing emotional effect.

It can sometimes be a challenge in minimalist photography to find the right balance when using colour to create visual interest. It is important not to overwhelm the image or detract from the minimalist aesthetic of simplicity.[2] The application of a certain colour palette or the emphasis on colour doesn't always have to be prominent. Instead, think about exploring muted tones and subtle variations, and the different emotions they can convey.

While vivid, brighter colours can be dramatic and visually compelling, and can also draw attention to an element, using them in a more understated way can work just as well with your minimalist compositions.[3] Interrupting a harmonious colour palette with a very small area of a complementary colour will be enough to introduce a focal point that stands out and breaks the monotony of a larger expanse of a single hue.[4]

[2] *See* Simplicity pp. 12–3
[3] *See* Vivid Colour pp. 56–7
[4] *See* Patterns and Repetition pp. 66–9

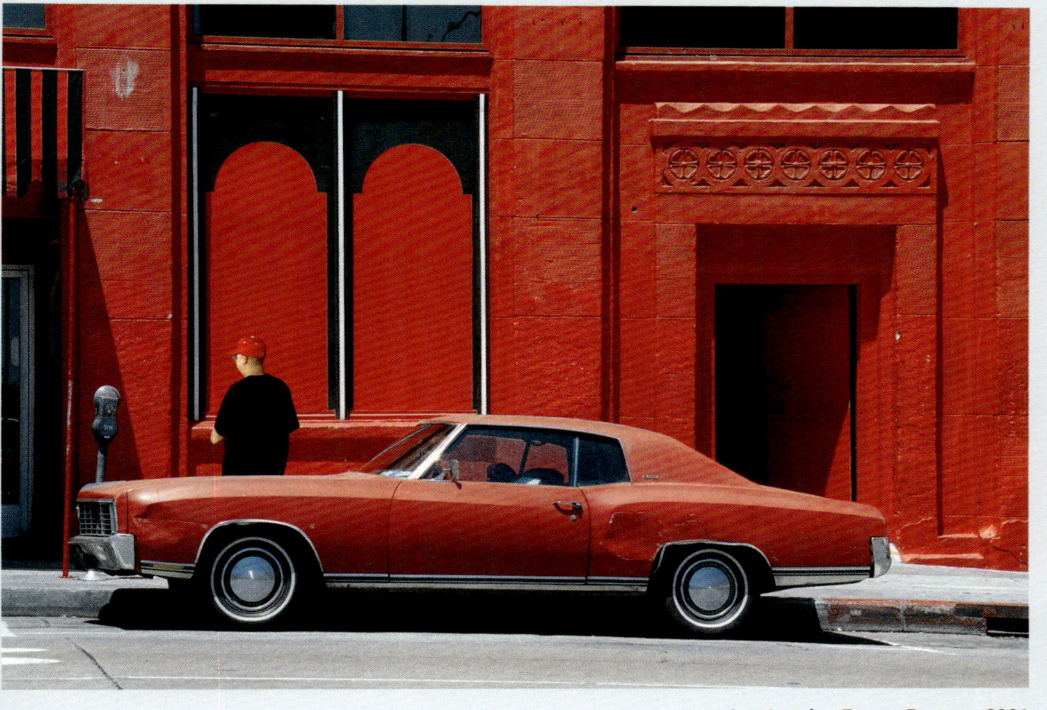

Los Angeles, Franco Fontana, 2001

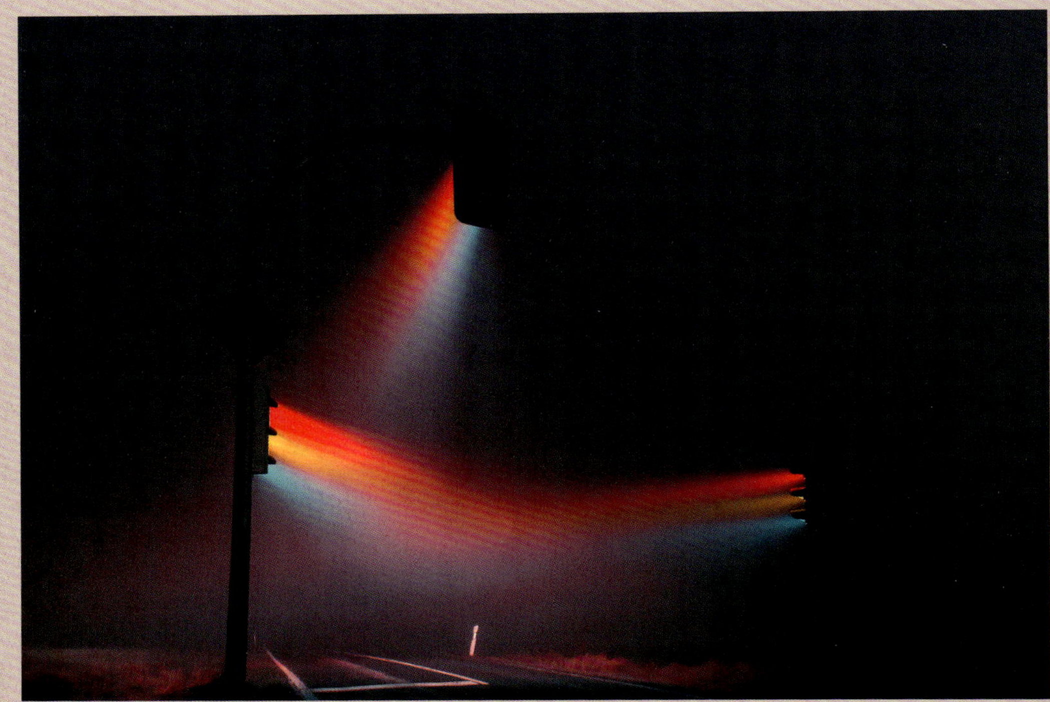

Traffic Lights Dark Side of The Earth, Lucas Zimmermann, 2013

VIVID COLOUR

USE BOLD HUES FOR ENERGY AND DEPTH

The inclusion of strong, vivid colours can play an interesting role in minimalist photography, helping to add depth and dimension to an otherwise simple composition.

Bright, vibrant colours in strategic key areas can guide the viewer through the frame and encourage them to explore the scene further. They introduce a dynamic element to a composition, creating points of interest that can draw attention to specific elements or the less obvious details in an image.[1] Using these vivid hues can also communicate directly with the viewer's emotions, influencing their mood and perception of a scene.

In this photograph, Lucas Zimmermann has created an atmospheric and mysterious image of traffic lights in dense fog. The rays of vibrant light take on an abstract appearance as they are diffused and softened by the haze, which transforms the mundane into a fleeting moment of surreal beauty. The radiant colours create a confusing portal into the unknown, inviting drivers to stop and proceed simultaneously. There is a feeling of suspense and trepidation from the surrounding darkness, while the spectral glow of the colourful lights creates mystical points of interest that demand visual attention.[2]

When you are creating your own minimalist compositions, consider how the careful selection of colours and their intensity and brightness can resonate in your images. Deciding how to include bright colours can have an immense impact on the overall image – a single burst of colour strategically placed against a neutral background, a dominant colour as a focal point and a gradual transition from one vibrant hue to another will all create very different effects in a scene.

The synergy between minimalist compositions and vivid colours is incredibly powerful. However, it is crucial to maintain simplicity. The boldness of the colour should not overwhelm the composition, but enhance it.

You can also play with colour in postproduction. A 'global' change will affect all the colours in the image, whereas a 'local' change will target a specific hue. Saturation affects the intensity of the colour, while luminosity refers to how bright or dark the colour seems. Reducing the latter will make colours appear richer yet darker. Extra care needs to be taken not to overdo these effects, however, as they can easily make the image appear unnatural and over-processed.

[1] *See* Focal Point pp. 28–9
[2] *See* Tension pp. 120–1

CREATIVE TECHNIQUES

GEOMETRIC FORMS

SEEK OUT SYMMETRICAL SHAPES AND PATTERNS

Geometric forms are defined by their clean lines, angles and symmetrical shapes, such as those found in circles, triangles and squares. These powerful elements are ideal for creating striking compositions in a minimalist image.[1]

Geometric forms can make compelling subjects in their own right, as these simple shapes can serve as strong focal points that naturally draw attention and provide a clear point of interest.[2] Their very nature epitomizes simplicity, with clean lines and instantly recognizable forms that are usually free of complexity. The use of geometric forms in a composition can also help to create a sense of balance and stability. Even in asymmetrical compositions they can suggest a sense of structural balance while retaining simplicity and focus.[3]

In this image I was looking to emphasize the stark details of the brutalist architecture. Its acute angles and dynamic angular shapes convey a real sense of power, energy and movement, despite being static. A simple, innate elegance can be found within these geometric forms, which gives the composition strong visual appeal.

The geometric shapes create contrast through their outlines, textures and tones, which are accentuated by the strong sunlight and pronounced angular shadows. The combination of precision and simplicity creates balance and draws attention, as the structure is reduced to its essential geometric form. The strong shapes against the clear sky transform the concrete structure into an almost abstract composition.

The use of geometry in minimalist images is not always about straightforward representation in a literal sense. Geometric shapes can be symbolic and used to convey meaning and emotion in an image. A circles is a universal symbol that often represents unity and feelings of completeness and continuity; squares and rectangles suggest stability, reliability and feelings of order and structure; triangles are dynamic shapes that – depending on their position – can convey feelings of strength or energy.[4]

Geometry is all around you, from the patterns formed by the spirals of seashells, to the cities and urban environments we live in. By focusing on the structure and form of an object or scene, you can create an image that is full of visual precision.

[1] *See* Visual Impact pp. 16–7
[2] *See* Focal Point pp. 28–9
[3] *See* Balance and Visual Weight pp. 14–5
[4] *See* Symbolism and Metaphor pp. 124–5

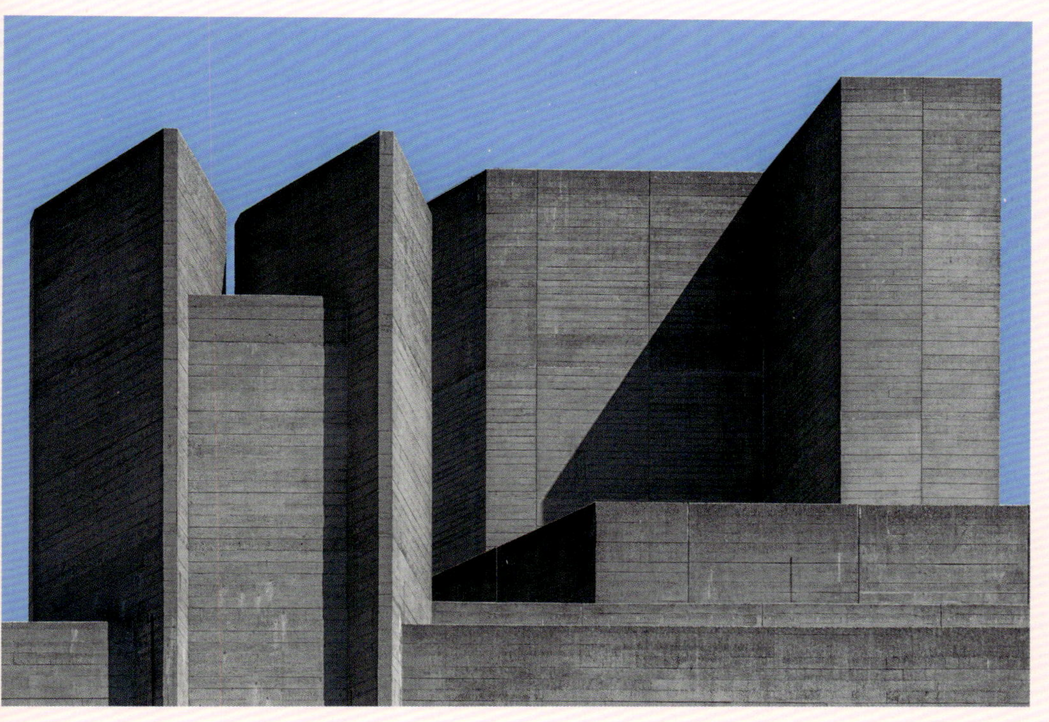

Brutalist Study IV, Antony Zacharias, 2018

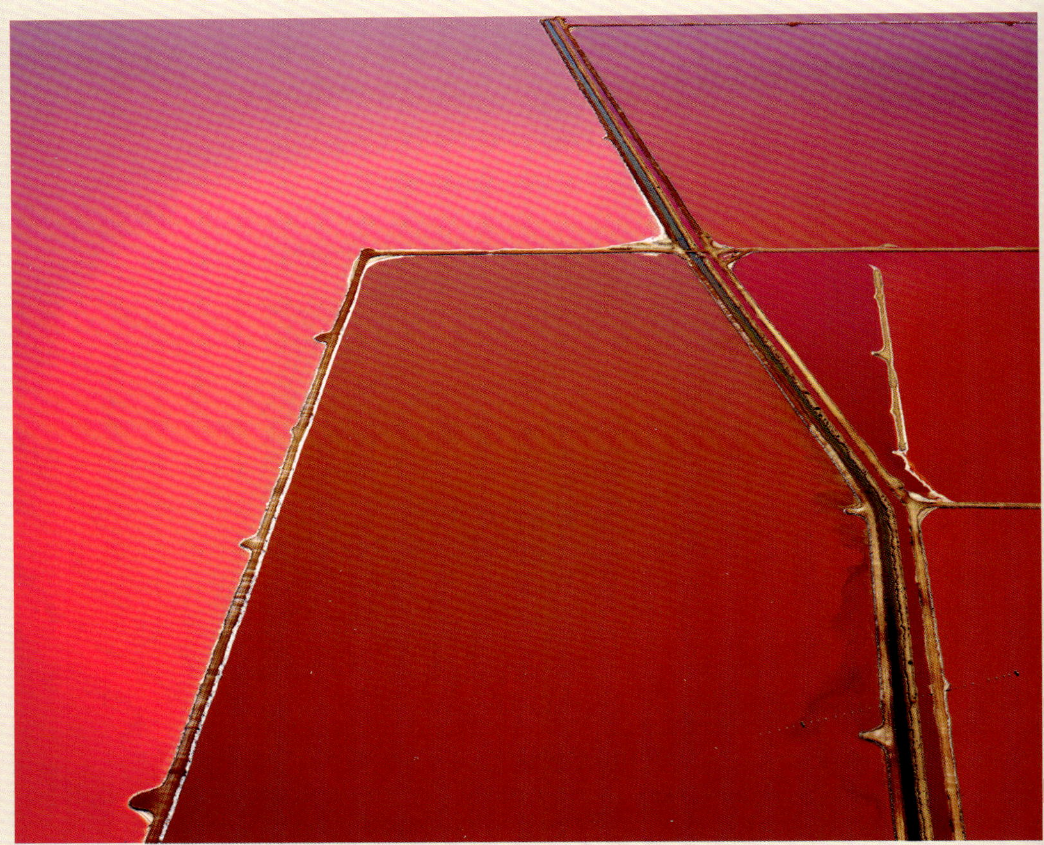

Pink Pools Hut Lagoon, David Burdeny, 2015

SHIFTING PERSPECTIVE

SHOOT FROM A DIFFERENT VANTAGE POINT

When we talk about perspective in photography, we are referring to the angle and position from which a photograph is taken. Shifting the perspective of a composition is about intentionally changing the way a scene is framed. The exploration of different viewpoints can transform the appearance of an image, not only in terms of the obvious changes that are made to its visual aesthetic, but by impacting the narrative layer and the viewer's engagement with it.

In this image, David Burdeny has photographed pink lagoons in Australia from a very high aerial perspective. Looking down from above, the image provides an expansive viewpoint that helps showcase the vastness and beauty of the area. The minimalist composition leverages the simplicity of form, colour and negative space, the roads adding depth and enhancing the sense of scale.[1] These human structures help us to appreciate the enormity of the terrain and reveal how it is part of a much larger environment.

Aside from changing your elevation, you can also experiment with unconventional camera angles and lateral movement, both of which can add a dynamic quality to a minimalist composition. Consider tilting your camera or repositioning it to view a subject from an unusual perspective, as this can enhance its abstract qualities and emphasize shapes, forms and lines.

Shifting perspective can also help to alter the narrative of a minimalist image by drawing attention to details that might have gone unnoticed from a conventional viewpoint. It can also introduce new contexts or appear to change an element's relationship with its environment. An unusual perspective can even create a sense of disorientation and unease in the viewer as they seek to understand and reconcile the image with their usual understanding of the scene.[2] For example, when composing an image, consider capturing your subject from the side rather than face-on. This can reveal different aspects of the subject and drastically alter its tone.

Playing with depth can also create something different and exciting; getting close to your subject will allow you to capture details and textures not visible from a distance. This can be achieved by physically changing position or by using a zoom lens.

Similarly, wider shots will include more of the environment in which you are photographing, which can help provide context and a sense of scale. A wide-angle lens can also exaggerate perspective, making close objects larger and those in the distance appear smaller.

[1] *See* Scale pp. 20–1
[2] *See* Visual Discord pp. 126–7

TEXTURES

BRING YOUR IMAGES ALIVE WITH TEXTURE

Gavin Goodman has incorporated pleated paper into this portrait to create a striking image, where both the paper and the graceful model form strong focal points. The textured paper adds complexity to the image by catching the light in a unique way.

Focusing on textures within a minimalist image can be a strong way to introduce an additional layer of depth and interest for the viewer. Including such a tangible quality not only conveys the essence of a subject, but also draws the audience in by providing a connection with the physicality of the scene.

However, incorporating textures in a minimal composition can be a delicate balance – when the priority is to convey the narrative in a simple and clear way, their inclusion should not over-complicate the image. Introducing a subtle texture can add a significant layer to a scene, as it will engage the viewer's senses beyond the visual and encourage a deeper exploration of the image. A more prominent inclusion of texture can also help in the visual narrative of an image. For example, the textured details of a weathered object can represent the passage of time, and imply resilience and strength, while the soft, ethereal textures created by mist and fog can evoke feelings of mystery and an atmosphere of intrigue and the unknown.[1]

Lighting can help highlight textures, so it pays to experiment with your camera angle and the positioning of any artificial lights to explore how this affects your image. Using manual focus, together with a tripod and remote shutter release, can prove invaluable when it comes to ensuring a sharp image. At the same time, pay attention to your aperture setting and depth of field because this will influence how the texture is captured – a smaller aperture (for greater depth of field) will result in more of the texture appearing in focus. You may also want to consider using a polarizing filter, which can help to reduce glare and enhance the saturation and contrast of the textures.

Textures also possess the ability to suggest emotions. By carefully selecting and emphasizing specific textures in a scene, you can lead the viewer to feel a certain way, even when there is a minimal aesthetic and simplistic composition. The inclusion of something soft can suggest comfort and warmth, for example, whereas a sharp, jagged or unpredictable texture may promote feelings of agitation or tension.

[1] *See* Symbolism and Metaphor pp. 124–5

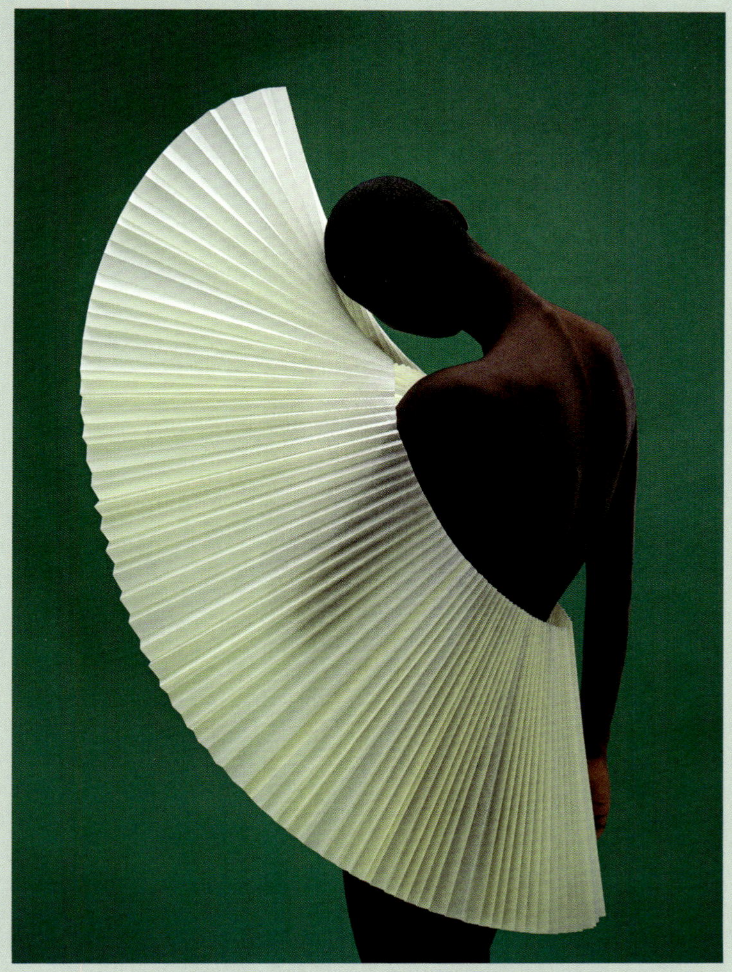

Luhlaza 3, Gavin Goodman, 2021

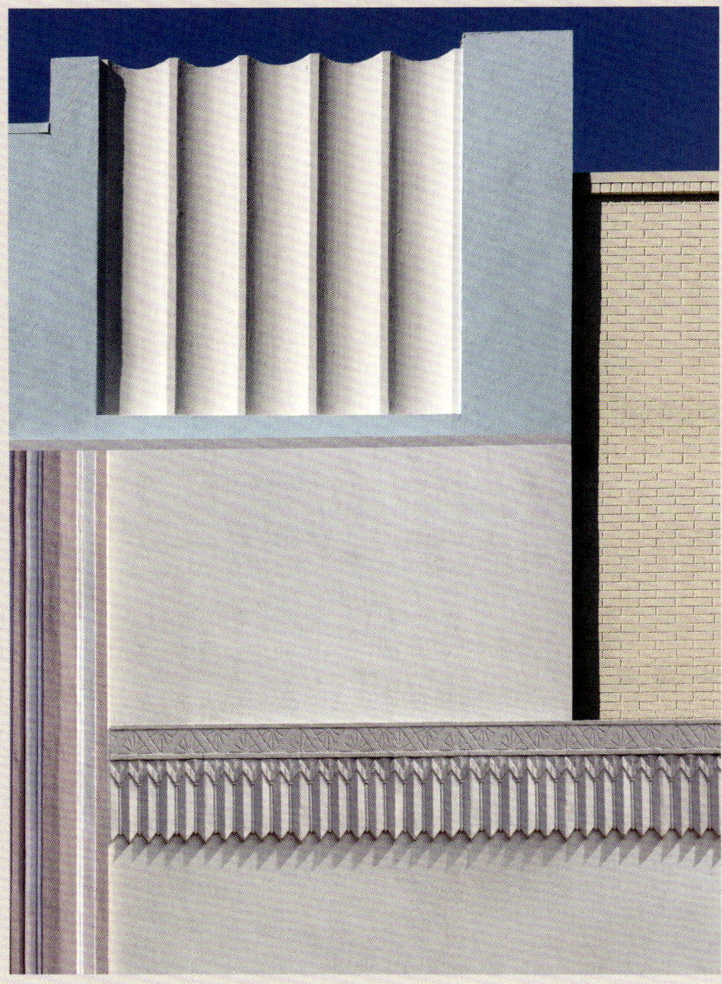

Architectural Design, Antony Zacharias, 2022

PATTERNS AND REPETITION

GIVE YOUR IMAGES A VISUAL RHYTHM

In this image, there are a number of different repeating patterns that work together to create a visually striking photograph. The minimalist composition focuses on the architectural details, clean lines and forms that help to give the patterns a central role. Light and shadow enhances certain elements, adding depth and dimension throughout, and the strong sunlight from the side helps to accentuate textures and create more defined patterns;[1] the contrasting yet muted colours and tones add visual interest that helps make the patterns appear more vivid and intense.[2] Finally, scale and proportion have a part to play, as the smaller repeating elements are as impactful as the larger patterns. Together, the elements gel in the composition to create a compelling graphic image.

Generally, patterns and repetition refer to the recurrence of specific visual elements in a way that creates a feeling or sense of order, rhythm or predictability within an image. The human mind is naturally drawn to patterns and repetition in art for several cognitive and psychological reasons. These preferences have deep-rooted connections to the way our brains process and interpret information and respond emotionally to it. Incorporating these repeating designs into a minimalist composition can serve multiple purposes, be it their aesthetic appeal or the way they invite thought through investigation and interpretation by the viewer.

Incorporating patterns and repetition successfully into a minimalist image requires a thoughtful approach. Composition is vital. Take the time to observe your surroundings and identify potential patterns or repeating elements. Consider how these may assist in the visual narrative of the image.[3] Simplicity is key and it is important to understand how the patterns are going to sit within your photograph – whether they are going to be the main focus, or simply an important element that helps explain the bigger picture.[4] Ask yourself how they assist the overall mood, feeling or theme of your image and its emotional impact. Remove any elements that don't contribute to the overall pattern or repetition that you want to highlight.

[1] *See* Shadows and Highlights pp. 46–7
[2] *See* Colour Palette pp. 52–3
[3] *See* Narrative in Composition pp. 130–3
[4] *See* Simplicity pp. 12–3

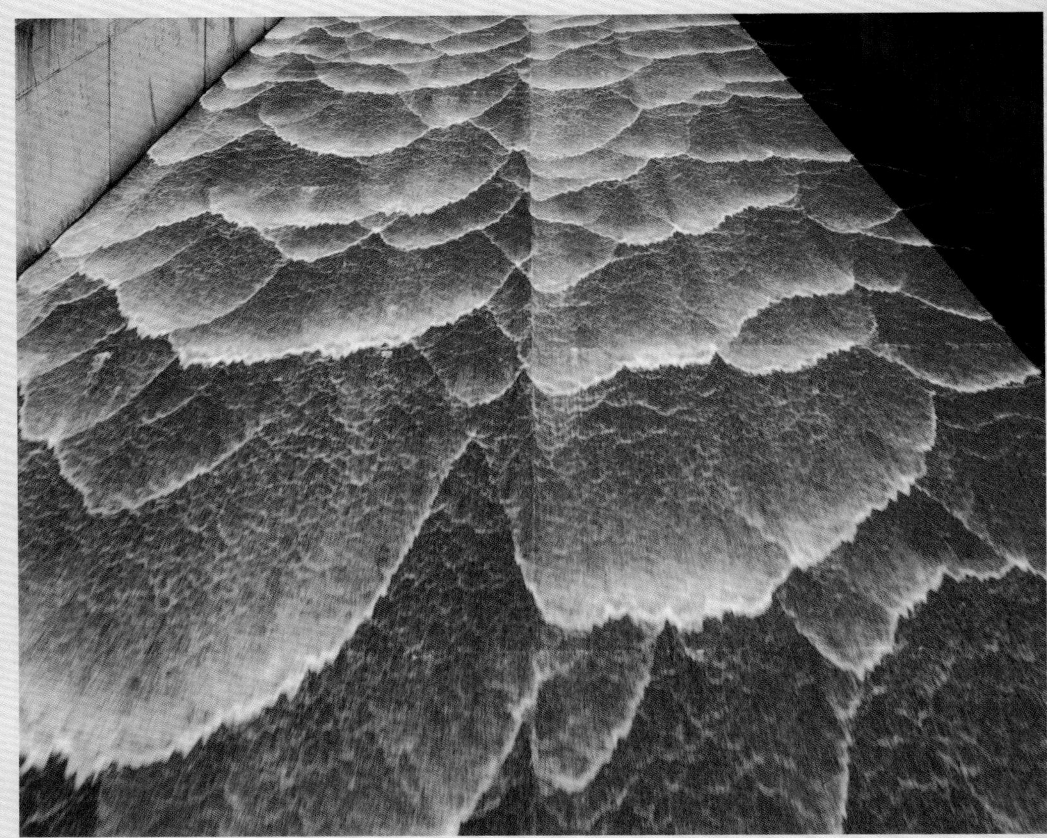

Obanazawa City, Yamagata Prefecture, Toshio Shibata, 2018

Playing with negative space may help to accentuate any potential patterns,[5] or you can consider incorporating them into your scene to achieve a harmonious composition. Likewise, see how different angles, positions and framing can reveal a more interesting pattern or repetition, or showcase those elements in a more effective way. Look for elements with contrasting colours, tones or textures that can add visual interest and make the patterns more defined and appealing.

Whether they are found in nature or human-made structures, patterns introduce a visual movement. The audience will find a sense of comfort and satisfaction in their predictability and order, and the recurring forms will create a visual flow that resonates with the viewer's subconscious. They can also become a visual anchor, grounding the viewer in a contemplative experience that goes beyond the surface of the photograph. When used deliberately and thoughtfully in a minimalist composition, this encourages viewers to explore the nuances within the frame and appreciate the subtle variations that emerge with each occurrence.

In this image, Toshio Shibata's use of repeated patterns creates a meditative viewing experience. The intentional simplification of the visual elements, together with the natural rhythms formed by the flowing water, establishes a hypnotic scene that invites viewers to engage in a moment of introspection. The absence of superfluous details allows the mind to focus on the essential, fostering a sense of tranquillity and mindfulness.[6] In a world inundated with visual stimuli, minimalist photography – enriched by patterns and repetition – offers respite. It provides a visual oasis that encourages reflection and connection.

Beyond their aesthetic appeal, patterns and repetition can help communicate themes of continuity, cycles and connection. Here, the natural patterns in the flowing water tell a silent tale of time and resilience.

[5] *See* Negative Space pp. 18–9

[6] *See* Tranquillity and Mindfulness pp. 116–7

SYMMETRY AND ASYMMETRY

CREATE A MIRROR IMAGE

In *Phillip II*, Mona Kuhn has balanced her image to form a harmonious unity within the frame. There is a clear use of symmetry in the arrangement of the composition and the placement of the elements. The symbiotic relationship between the subjects is immediately visible and resonates a visual simplicity, while simultaneously emphasizing the beauty found in the intentional alignment of the bodies. The lack of complexity fosters a sense of tranquillity and invites the viewer to contemplate and engage with the image on a deeper level.

Symmetry refers to the arrangement of visual elements in a composition where one part of the image is reflected or mirrored by another. It is a key technique in minimalist photography, where the emphasis is often on achieving balance and order.[1] Because of this, symmetry can have a major influence on how the viewer engages with a photograph and a fundamental impact on how they are guided through the composition.

The symmetry within an image is characterized by a general balance of some of the main elements. Compositionally, this can be achieved in several ways: through the intentional placement of objects, or the inclusion and deliberate emphasis on other elements, such as reflections, patterns or other arrangements that are found within the scene.

Conversely, asymmetry – the deliberate offsetting of the arrangement of elements – can radically alter the natural feelings of tranquillity and peace, and replace them with intense opposites. The lack of symmetry can create tension and discomfort, and place additional emphasis on the individual parts of the frame. This, in turn, raises questions as to why they were included and their role in the image.[2]

[1] *See* Balance and Visual Weight pp. 14–5
[2] *See* Tension pp. 120–1

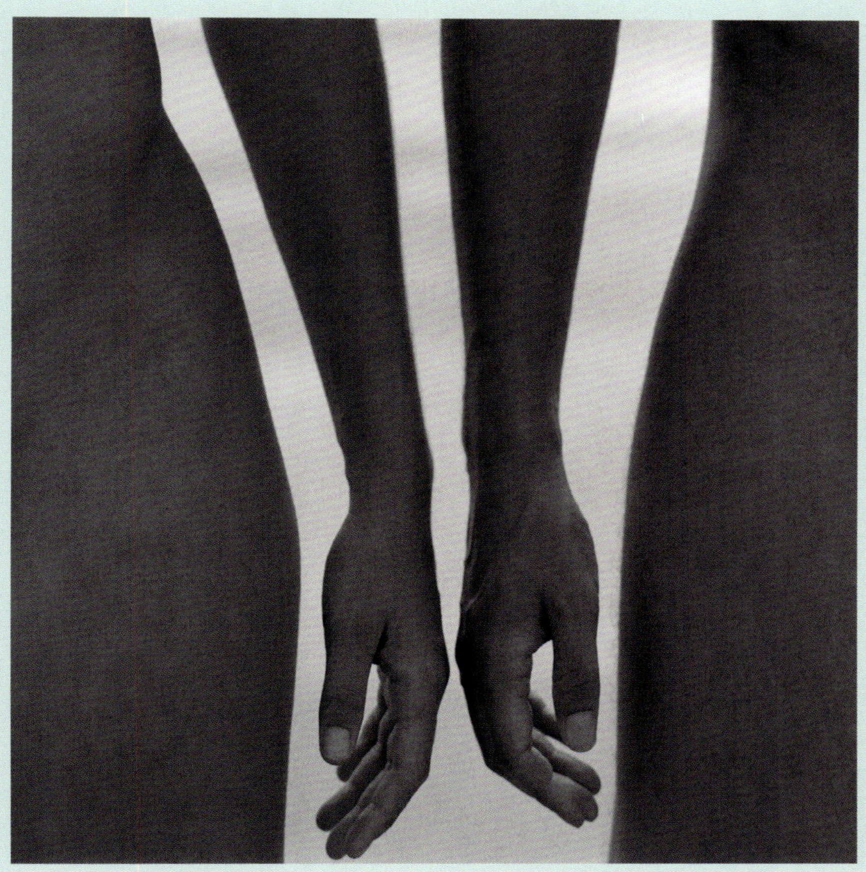

Phillip II, Mona Kuhn, 1997

The placement of the elements in Hiroshi Sugimoto's composition opposite deliberately challenges the viewer's expectations. This image seemingly represents two moonlit trees under a partially cloudy night sky but is in fact an imprint of an electrical current on photographic film, taken in a darkened studio. By playing with scale and deliberately leaving negative space around the elements, the photographer has created a powerful and thought-provoking image. The irregularity of the asymmetrical composition has a profound influence. We are immediately drawn to the brightest elements, which are off-centre and imbalanced, and this leads us to explore the image with a feeling of tension. These feelings are emphasized by their jagged, irregular form.

Visual harmony is often considered a key component in a strong and powerfully engaging minimalist photograph. When a scene is reduced to its core essential elements, there is a natural sense of order that becomes a guide to help direct the viewer to the emotional heart of the picture. The audience will follow these visual cues and seek to understand and interpret what they see, and possibly consider what is missing. Symmetry can be used as an aid to reduce this visual complexity, by eliminating unnecessary and distracting details. When thoughtfully included in an image, it can also help draw attention to the essence of the subject and assist in creating a strong connection between the viewer and the story.

We naturally find symmetry visually appealing, as it promotes a perceived feeling of stability, security, calm and unity in a composition. However, breaking an obvious symmetry can often foster a deeper and more elaborate connection with the photograph. This is especially true when an image challenges the expected beauty found in balance and order and replaces it with something more unique and unpredictable; it can seem more appealing and engaging because it reflects the complexity of the real world. This deviation from the symmetrical introduces a dynamic and unsettled quality that can evoke feelings of energy, disparity, tension and fascination, as your audience seeks to understand and decipher the image.

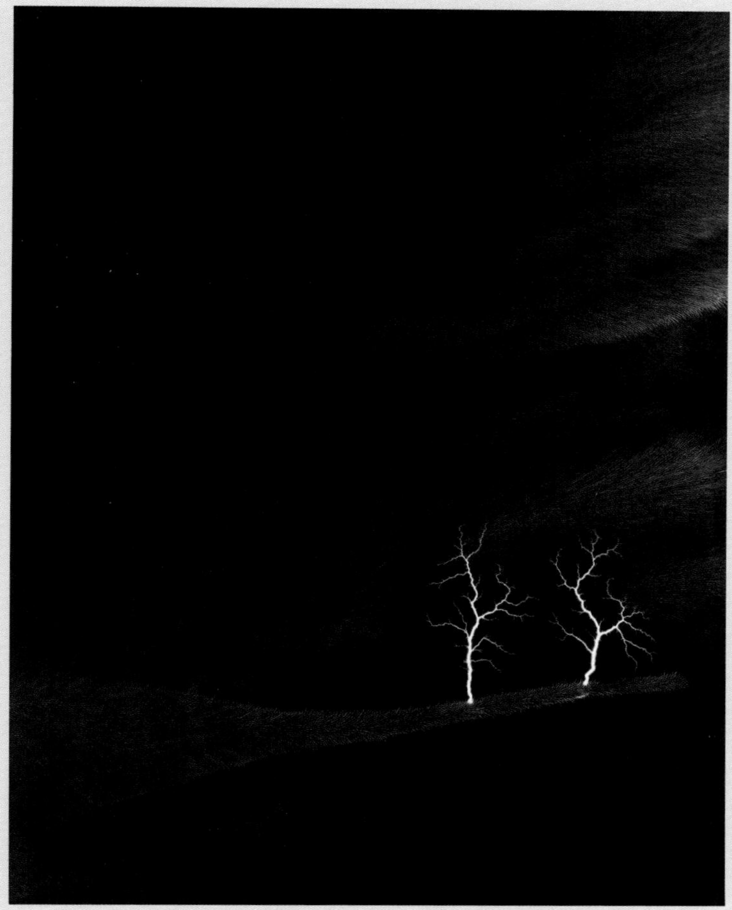

Lightning Fields 144, Hiroshi Sugimoto, 2009

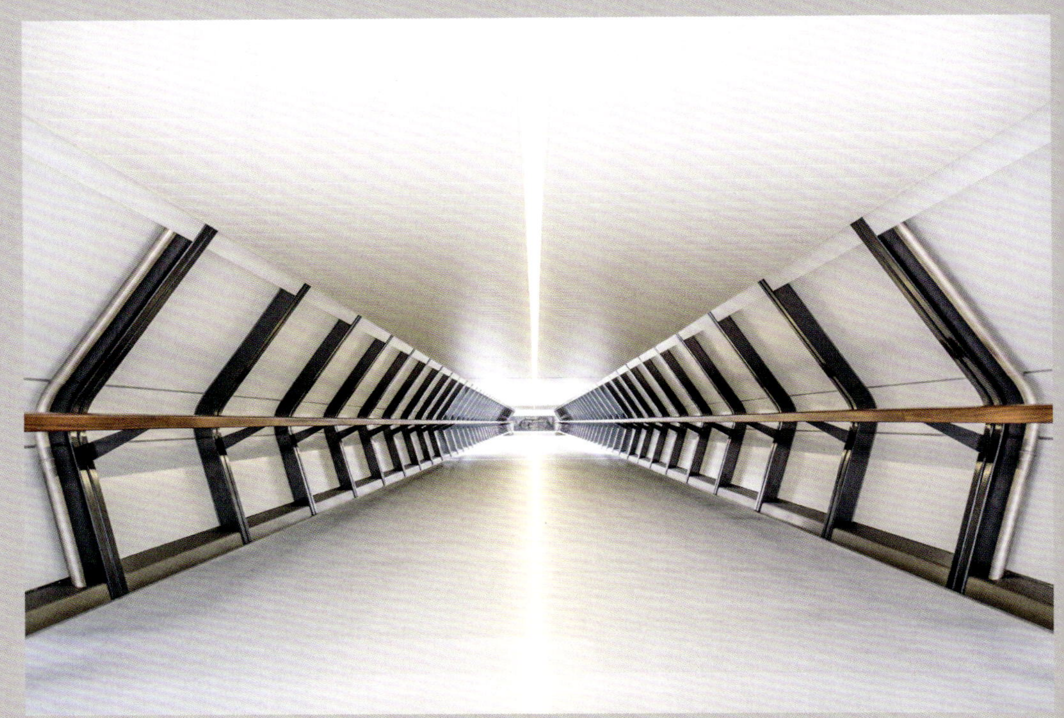

The Walkway, Antony Zacharias, 2015

LINES AND PATHWAYS

LEAD YOUR VIEWER BY THE HAND

This image of a modern, urban walkway uses the power of lines to create a striking, yet simple minimalist image. The interaction of the different lines creates an energetic flow and movement that infuses an otherwise static image with feelings of vitality. Strong diagonal, horizontal, vertical and curved lines unite to create a balanced and pleasing composition. The natural rhythm suggested by the repeating linear patterns results in areas of tension and release. The high-key lighting softens the lines and reduces contrast, adding a suggestion of calm and guiding the eye.[1]

The inclusion of lines – and the suggested visual pathways that can be created with them – is fundamental in minimalist photographic compositions. They can help to create structure and depth, as well as directing attention within an otherwise simple photograph.

In minimalist photography, incorporating lines can convey a sense of direction and movement.[2] Naturally, different types of line serve a slightly different purpose and evoke a distinct feeling. Straight lines elicit stability, order and simplicity, whereas curved lines suggest softness, comfort and elegance. Curved lines also appear more relaxed, and the viewer will usually follow the curve at a slower pace.

Diagonal lines can introduce a feeling of movement and power in an image, and seemingly control how your audience follows them through the scene. They convey action and appear livelier and more energetic than vertical or horizontal lines. Jagged, broken and irregular lines will often make the viewer feel unsettled and uncomfortable as they try to follow them through a composition.

[1] *See* High Key pp. 38–9
[2] *See* Directing Emotion pp. 92–3

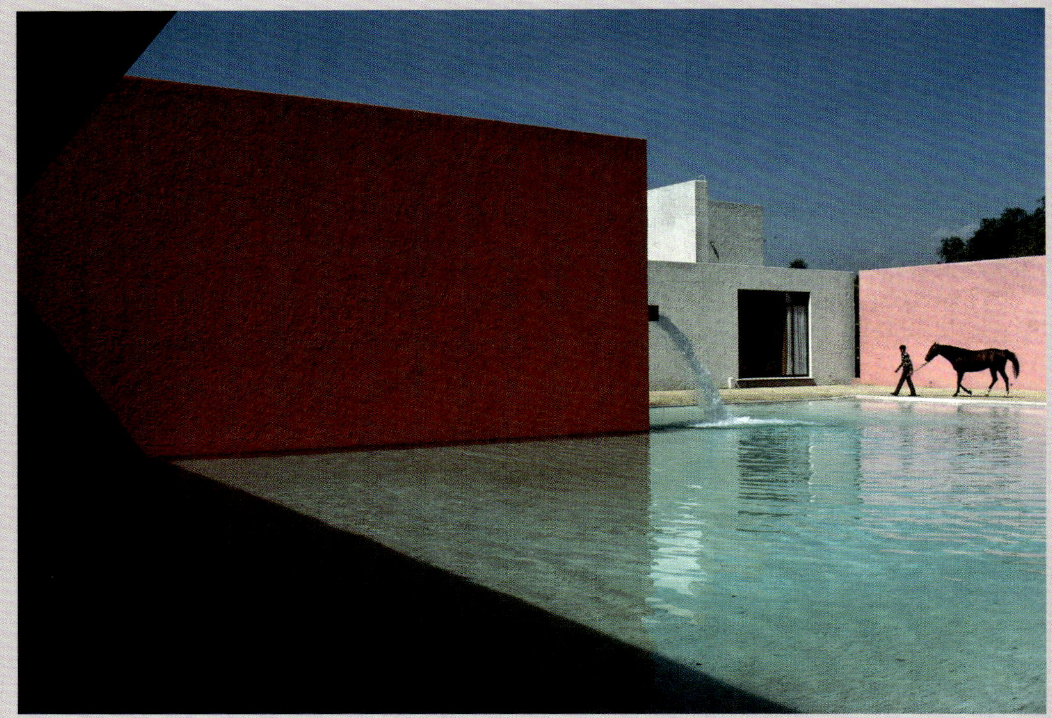

Horse Stable Pool, Mexico, Architects: Luis Barragan and Andres Casillas, Mexico City, René Burri, 1976

Despite being less apparent or obvious, pathways can also play a crucial role as a visual guide. These are subtle, yet powerful elements that invite the viewer to journey through a photograph. With careful application and arrangement, you can direct the audience along a deliberate route towards the key elements that you want them to consider.

These pathways can be literal and obvious – such as a track or river meandering through a scene – or they can be implied by the careful positioning of objects or the use of colour, shape, contrast and shadows. Determining where the pathway will lead, its shape and how it transcends the surrounding elements will all affect how the viewer engages with the image.

René Burri has utilized a combination of lines and visual pathways to subtly control and guide us through this image. Our eye naturally 'enters' the scene at the bottom-centre, at the compelling diagonal that bisects the water with a powerful leading line of dark shadow. At its intersection with the strong, graphic red wall, our gaze immediately changes direction and we follow this line towards the waterfall, onto the doorway and then further around to rest at the silhouetted forms of the person and horse positioned against the pastel pink wall. This journey seemingly happens in an instant, but by the time we arrive at the main subjects of the image, we have taken in numerous other elements. These have all been positioned carefully in the composition so that they not only lead us to the man and the horse, but also help us understand the story behind the image itself.

Lines and pathways are more than just compositional elements in a minimalist photograph. Carefully considering their position and arrangement in the frame will have a profound effect on the overall tone of the image. They can act as subtle or obvious visual cues that impact the dynamics of an image depending on how they guide the viewer (and the fluidity of this movement), how they elicit emotions and ultimately how they enhance the minimalist aesthetic of the photograph.

ORGANIC SHAPES

FIND BEAUTY IN THE IRREGULAR

Organic shapes are more fluid and generally more irregular and unpredictable than regular geometric forms.[1] While they are sometimes found in artificial and human-made elements, these shapes are more commonly found within the natural world. When included in minimalist compositions they can add an additional layer of complexity and emotion to an image.

Rather than merely defining what the viewer sees, organic forms introduce a sense of tactile emotion through suggestion and impression. Compared to more linear and regular geometric forms, these shapes often appear softer and less imposing. They can suggest beauty in imperfection. These irregular shapes and curves can help to moderate compositions, adding a subtle softness and fluidity.

The image shown here focuses on the organic shape and form of a fern frond. There is a balance and harmony in the image that is created through the plant's symmetry, which showcases the natural shapes that create intricate repeating patterns.[2] The plant has been photographed close up and isolated against a black background, which helps draw attention to the intricate beauty of its organic shapes. The repetitive patterns are visually striking and invite the viewer to explore the texture and details of the plant.

Shapes generally provide the outline and contours that define what we see; a subject is often a shape or is defined by a collection of shapes. Organic forms are usually more abstract and individual, which makes them more open to interpretation by the viewer.[3]

When you are incorporating organic shapes into a minimalist composition, consider the complexity of the natural form and how it will interact with other elements in the frame. It is vital to ensure that the shapes don't detract from the clean, minimalist aesthetic of simplicity, and it is also important to maintain a sense of balance and harmony throughout the image. Evaluate how different lighting can transform the shapes you include by casting shadows and helping to define textures and form.

Your choice of colour palette will also affect how organic shapes are represented in your image. A vibrant colour palette can energize shapes, for example, while softer, more muted tones – or a monochrome treatment – can highlight form and texture, and emphasize the natural elegance of the shapes.[4]

[1] *See* Geometric Forms pp. 60–1
[2] *See* Patterns and Repetition pp. 66–9
[3] *See* Abstracts pp. 84–5
[4] *See* Colour Palette pp. 52–5

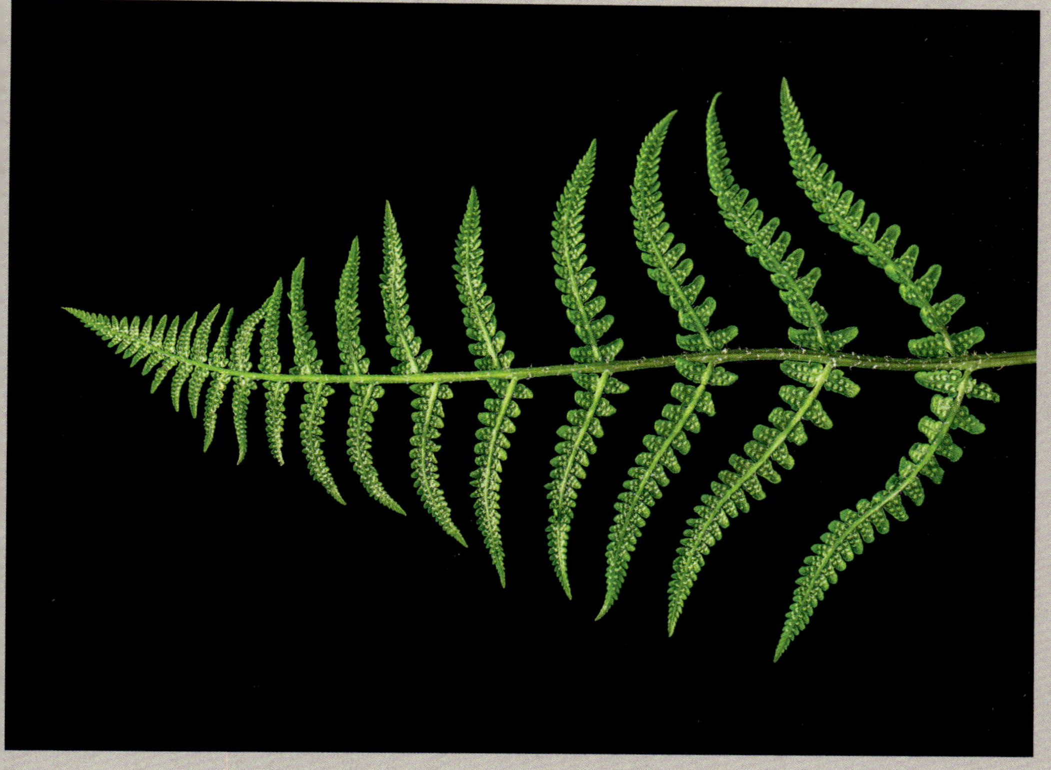

Frond, Antony Zacharias, 2014

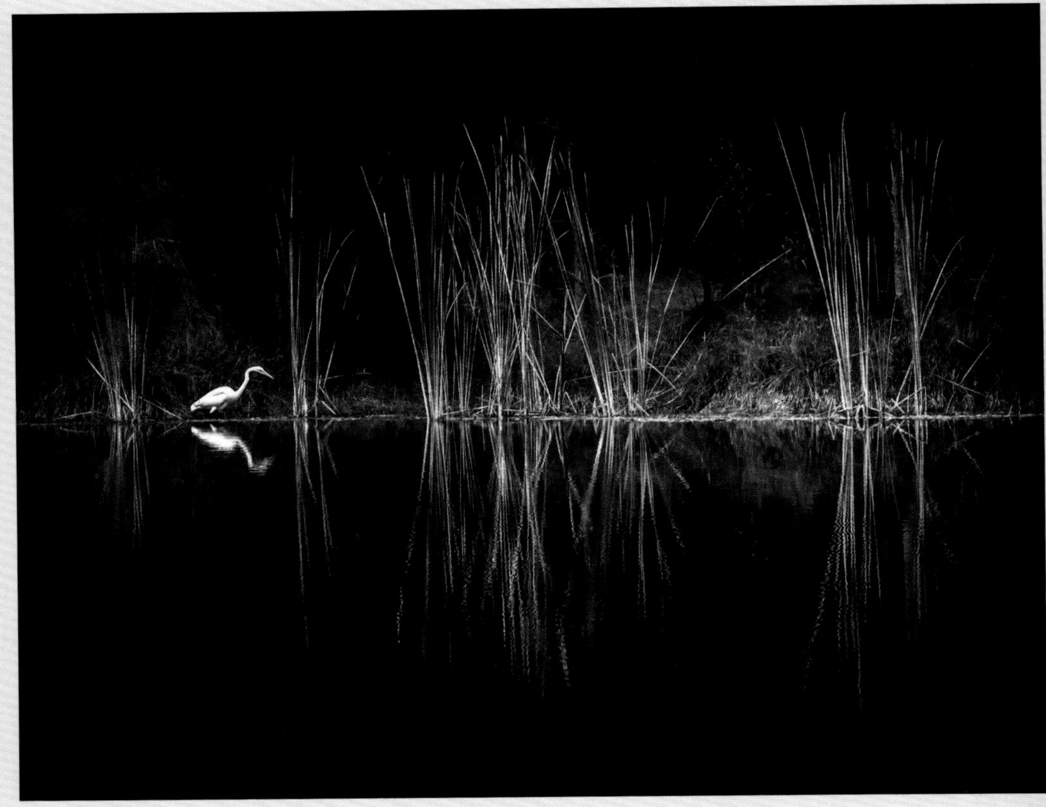

Egret, Antony Zacharias, 2010

REFLECTIONS

DOUBLE THE IMPACT WITH A REFLECTIVE SURFACE

Reflections are essentially a mirrored version of a part or the whole of a scene, which can add depth and interest to an image, while retaining a simplistic minimalist approach. Visual balance is a cornerstone of minimalist photography, and including a reflection is a natural way to achieve symmetry in a composition.[1] Mirrored elements can create a sense of equilibrium that not only achieves a sense of harmony and balance but is also visually appealing to the viewer. The symmetry of the reflection doesn't have to be perfect: an incomplete mirrored image can still double the impact of the subject without overwhelming it.[2] Similarly, subtle variations between elements and their reflections can create an additional layer of interest for an audience.

The reflections on the still water of the lake in this scene provided an excellent opportunity to capture a striking minimalist photograph. The visual impact of the solitary egret fishing among the reeds and tall grasses is doubled by the reflections, yet there is a harmonious symmetry where the image is split in half. The reflections in the water retain the minimalist aesthetic and evoke feelings of calm and serenity. A black-and-white treatment enhances the mood and minimizes distractions, naturally amplifying the contrast between the subject and its surroundings to make it appear more prominent in the frame.[3]

Reflections can accentuate key elements and draw the viewer's attention towards a specific subject. They can also create surreal, abstract compositions that challenge the viewer's perception of reality and illusion.[4] This can be a subtle approach that adds a layer of depth and complexity to the image, or a more dramatic treatment that introduces a sense of mystery through highly distorted and ambiguous shapes.

[1] *See* Balance and Visual Weight pp. 14–5
[2] *See* Symmetry and Asymmetry pp. 70–3
[3] *See* Monochrome pp. 50–1
[4] *See* Abstracts pp. 84–5

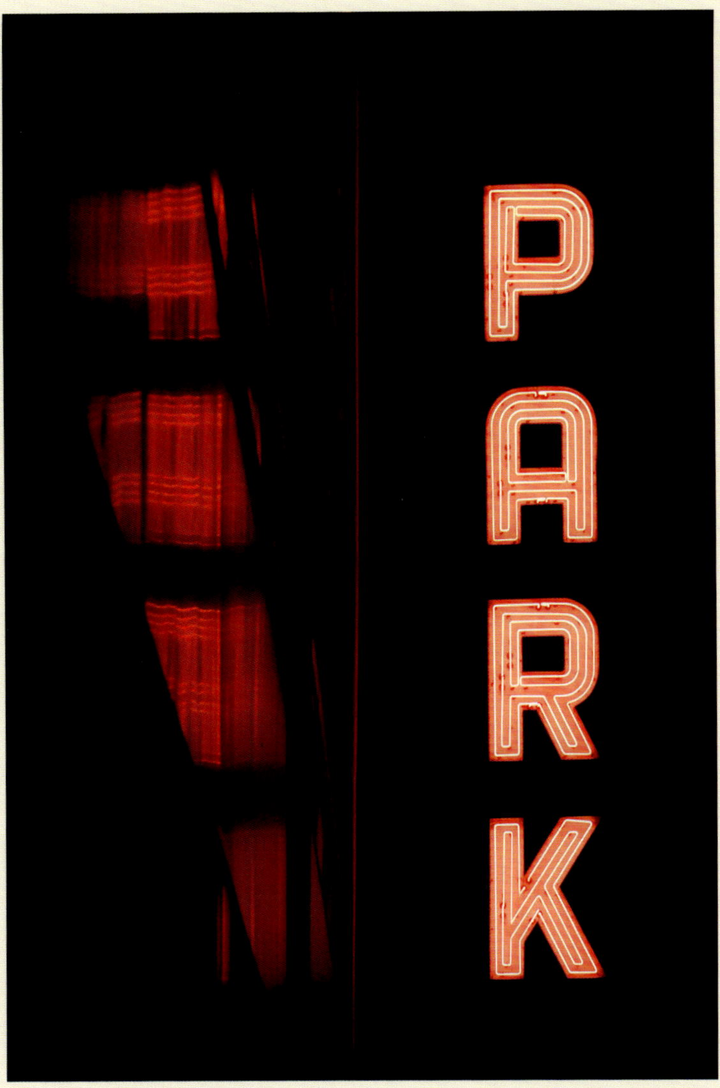

Park NYC, Antony Zacharias, 2008

Naturally, any reflective surface will create a mirrored effect, but the key is to consider your composition carefully. Look for elements that create interesting forms and lines when they are reflected and experiment with your framing and camera position. Play with different angles, viewpoints and perspective to see what effect this has on the reflective surface and other elements in the frame.

Pay close attention to the light, as the angle of light is essential in determining how and where reflections appear and interact in the frame. The strength of the light is also influential: soft, diffused light will create gentle, subtle reflections that create feelings of serenity and peace, while harsh, direct light will produce more pronounced reflections that convey strength, drama or perhaps isolation.

This image of a car park's neon sign uses a more subdued mirrored reflection, capturing the light cast on the side of a building. The minimalist composition draws attention through its visual impact, which is combined with artistic expression. The reflected red hues add a layer of interest and provide a balance that encourages the viewer to look beyond the main 'subject' in the photograph, creating a sense of space that extends across the image. Shot in low light conditions, a wide aperture and high ISO helped brighten the exposure, resulting in a crisp, clear image. Ultimately, the position and angle of the mirrored reflections create a unique composition and lend the image a cinematic feel and timeless quality.

ABSTRACTS

CAPTURE SOMETHING OUT OF CONTEXT

An immediate power and energy is evident in William Klein's image, combined with a feeling of distortion and chaos. The dramatic shapes and their fading, blurred counterparts combine to alter the perspective of what it is we are seeing.[1] There is a real sense of movement, yet also a stillness, and both sit together in the frame. The boldness of the dominant shapes and the use of strong angles and contrast creates a unique visual narrative.

An abstract photograph is not seeking to be a true or accurate representation of reality. Instead, the viewer is invited to engage with a less obvious image and to interpret what they see using their imagination and thought in an individual and subjective way.

There are almost limitless ways in which you can create an abstract photograph. It is a personal journey where the subject, elements or scene can be completely or partially disguised and shrouded in mystery. The way in which shapes, colours, contrast, light and shadow interact can all be used as a start for your minimalist abstract journey. The way you choose to hide the literal and decide what to reveal – and in what form – will encourage the audience to use their imagination. They will naturally draw upon their own personal experiences as they seek to interpret and understand your photograph, creating a strong connection as they do so.

You are also free to experiment with traditional camera settings. What are the effects of using different shutter speeds and different apertures? If you play with intentional blur, how does this affect the feeling and aesthetic of your image? The placement of elements in the frame can dramatically alter the mood of an image, but as with all minimalist photographs it is the absence of distraction and unnecessary information that is key, so allow space for your ideas to develop.

Regardless of your subject matter, the way you feel when you capture an image – and how you choose to express those feelings within your photograph – will have a direct impact on your viewer's engagement and interpretation of it. Ask yourself what kind of connection will be made. Will it be one of elegance, grace and restraint, or something more powerful, dominant and imposing?

[1] *See* Blur pp. 94–5

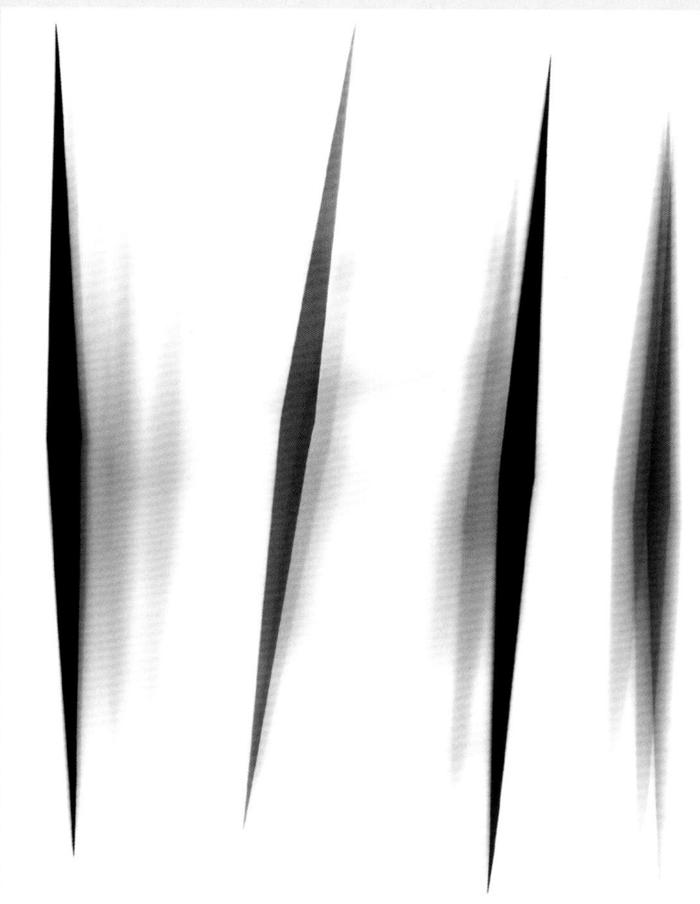

Abstract #6, Paris, William Klein, 1952

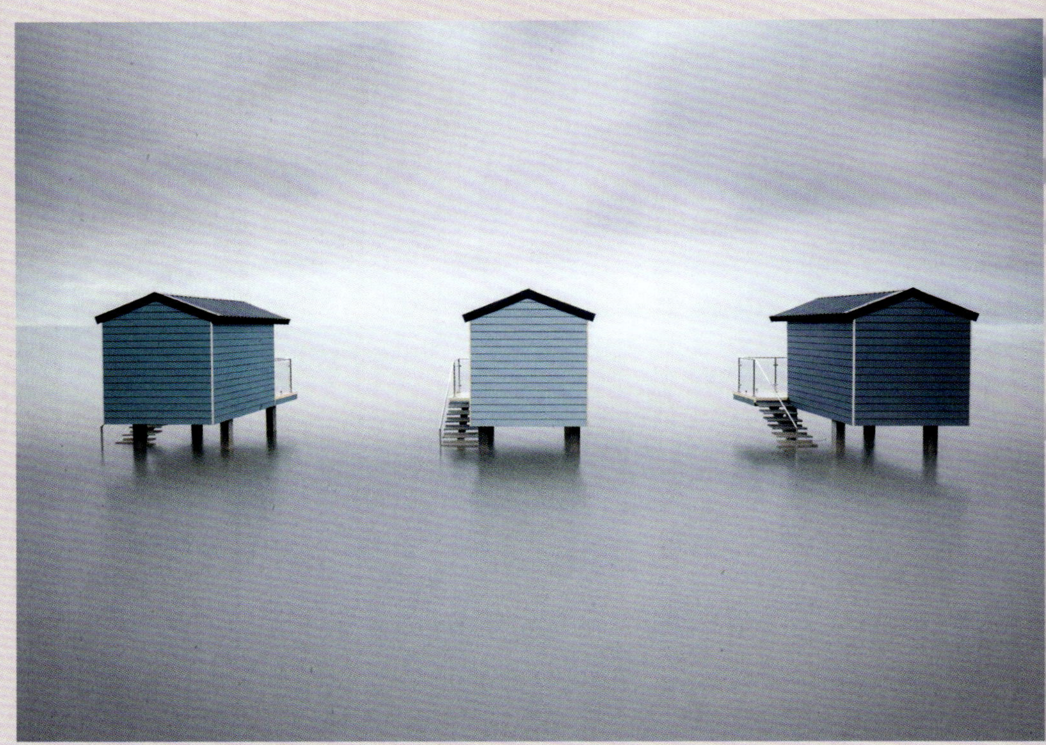

Fishing Huts, Antony Zacharias, 2018

LONG EXPOSURE

CREATE MAGICAL SHOTS BY EXTENDING TIME

Long exposures provide you with an opportunity to create images that explore time and motion in a composition. The camera's shutter is left open for an extended period, beyond what is ordinarily required for a 'correct' exposure. Combined with a minimalist composition this opens up a fascinating realm of possibilities. Capturing static and moving elements together can introduce a sense of wonderment that challenges perceptions of time and space, and captures ordinary moments that would otherwise go unnoticed.

Extending the exposure time can help to reduce a scene to its core elements and simplify busy compositions. This can effectively highlight any static elements and create a sense of isolation and focus on the subject. However, integrating long exposures into minimalist images requires careful consideration of the subject matter. Think about which elements are stationary and which are transient and will be blurred – or perhaps even erased – from the image during the longer exposure.

A long exposure combined with a minimalist composition can produce arresting images that evoke strong feelings of tranquillity and peace.[1] In this image, three fishing huts stand in deliberate isolation on a misty morning. A neutral density filter enabled a very long shutter speed to be used, which flattened and smoothed the moving water, removing any ripples and other distractions from the scene. Similarly, the flowing clouds have been transformed into soft wispy streaks.[2]

The central position of the huts adheres to the principles of simplicity and balance, and allows the structures to take centre stage. The emptiness around them becomes a powerful visual element, and this negative space encourages the viewer to contemplate the tranquil landscape.[3]

The easiest way to extend your exposure times is to switch your camera to Aperture Priority or Manual mode and dial in the lowest ISO setting and a small aperture, such as f/16. If this doesn't result in a slow enough shutter speed (or you want to use a wider aperture setting for a shallow depth of field) consider using a neutral density filter to extend your exposure times. In either case, you need to ensure your camera doesn't move during the exposure, so use a stable tripod or place your camera on a solid surface and trigger it remotely – you want the blur in your images to come from the movement of your subject, not from inadvertent camera shake.

[1] *See* Tranquillity pp. 116–7
[2] *See* Movement pp. 88–91
[3] *See* Negative Space pp. 18–9

MOVEMENT

CAPTURE A FLEETING MOMENT

Capturing stillness is often closely associated with the aesthetic of simplicity, and therefore with minimalist photography. However, suggesting a sense of movement can give your photographs a dynamic dimension. Whether it's freezing a fleeting instant or capturing a longer moment, the integration of movement can transform how an image is perceived.

In minimalist photography, incorporating a feeling of movement is about introducing subtle, deliberate actions that emphasize the transience of time and capture the essence of a moment, adding life and energy to your composition. When experimenting with movement, it is important to consider how it enhances the narrative of the image and what is the right amount; it can be easy to overwhelm a scene with chaotic motion.

Another benefit to incorporating movement in your photographs is the ability to evoke emotion and engage the viewer. Deciding whether to freeze a moment or emphasize the motion of events is the primary decision, and both will affect how the viewer feels about your image. The direction, speed and nature of the movement will all impact the feeling of the image: slow, smooth movements can create a sense of peace and calm, while fast, sharper movements evoke urgency and energy.

Freezing motion – where the subject is captured in sharp detail suspended in a specific moment – is an effective technique when you want to preserve a split second of intense activity. Together with a minimalist composition it can help you preserve the clarity of the elements and accentuate the inherent stillness of your subject. Technically, a fast shutter speed and appropriate lighting will enable you to capture high-speed motion, although you may need to increase the ISO setting and/or use a wider aperture to ensure the shutter speed is fast enough. This will ensure that the subject is sharply defined and free of any motion blur that might compromise the clarity of the moment.

In this image, Philippe Halsman froze the movement of the subject – a diver – rendering them motionless with sharp precision. There is a perfect stillness in the frame that captures the fleeting moment with both elegance and a sense of tranquillity. The resulting image is a visual meditation that invites the viewer to contemplate and appreciate the simplicity that is inherent in the stillness.

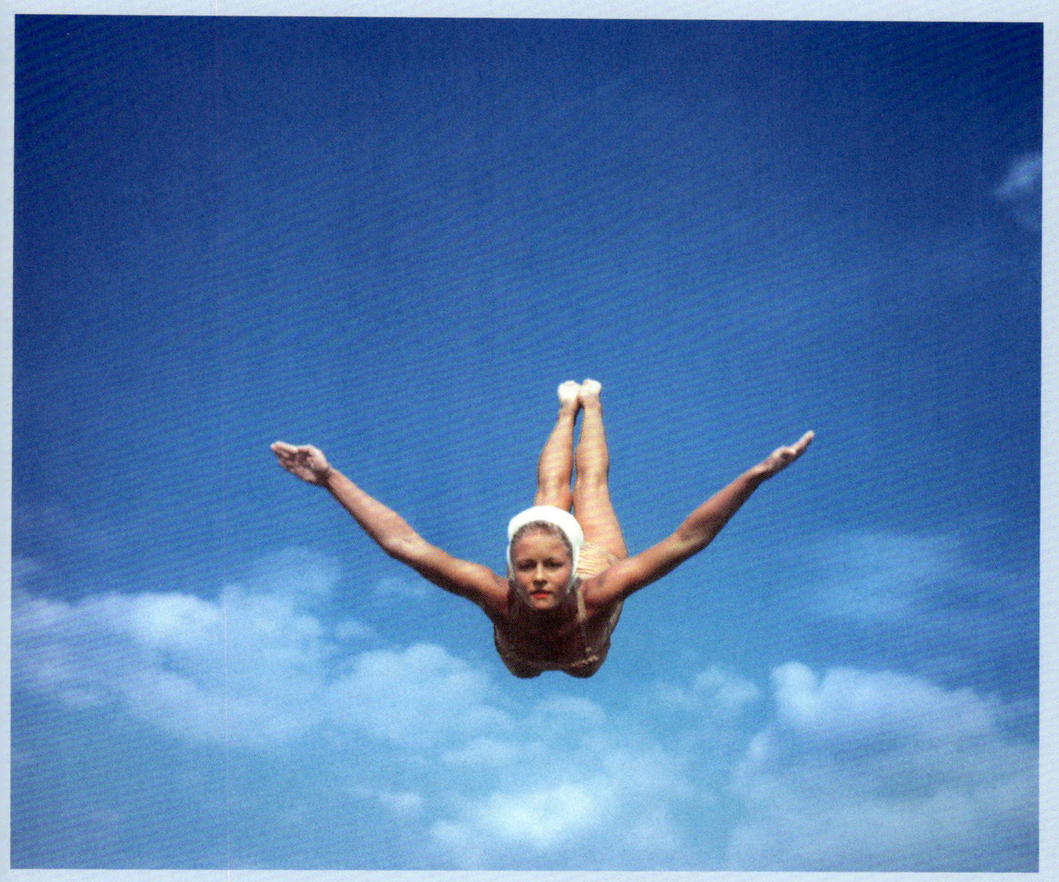

Champion Diver Lynn Morrison, Philippe Halsman, 1954

Conversely, employing slow shutter speeds provides you with the opportunity to portray movement in a very different way. Condensing a longer period into a two-dimensional image can result in a photograph with a strong sense of fluidity and a dreamlike serenity.[1] Here, Alexey Titarenko utilized a slow shutter speed to capture the movement of the crowds blurred as ghostlike forms. This lends the image an abstract and dreamlike quality, which contrasts with the stationary young boy. Not only does this static figure add stability – which accentuates the sense of movement – but he is captured looking directly at the camera, which creates a stronger emotional connection with the audience.

Capturing the essence of movement (or stillness) is a decisive way of enhancing visual interest in your minimalist images. By layering the perception of time and space within the frame, viewers will be invited to explore the relationship between the moving and static elements. Including elements in motion – be it through intentional blur, emphasizing the trajectory of a subject or freezing a split-second moment – can convey a powerful story. These alternative approaches provide you with the opportunity to direct the storytelling and develop visually compelling narratives.[2]

It is challenging to balance the sense of motion and stillness, but it is essential that neither one overpowers the minimalist aesthetic. They require careful timing and thought when it comes to composition and exposure to ensure they complement the simplicity of the scene and the content and story of the image.

[1] *See* Long Exposure pp. 86–7
[2] *See* Narrative in Composition pp. 130–3

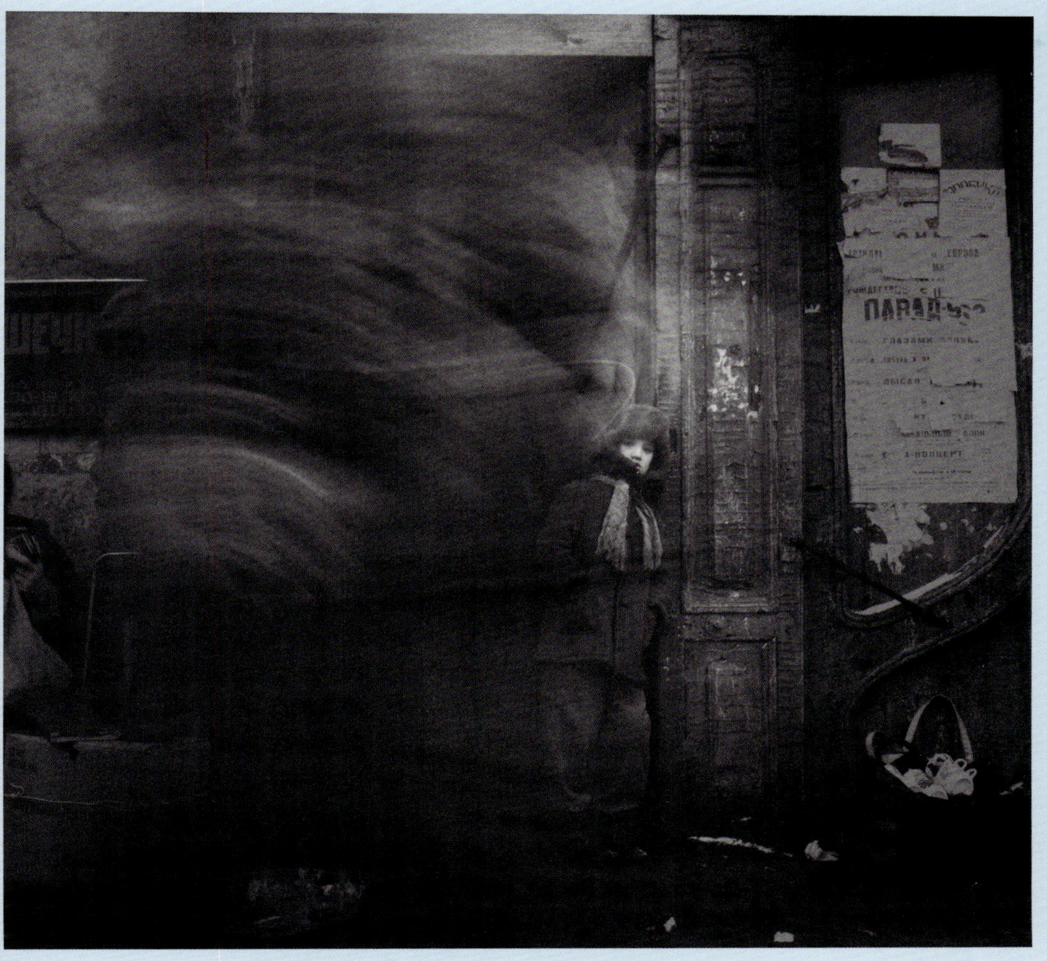

Homeless Boy, Street Market, St. Petersburg, from the *City of Shadows* series, Alexey Titarenko, 1993

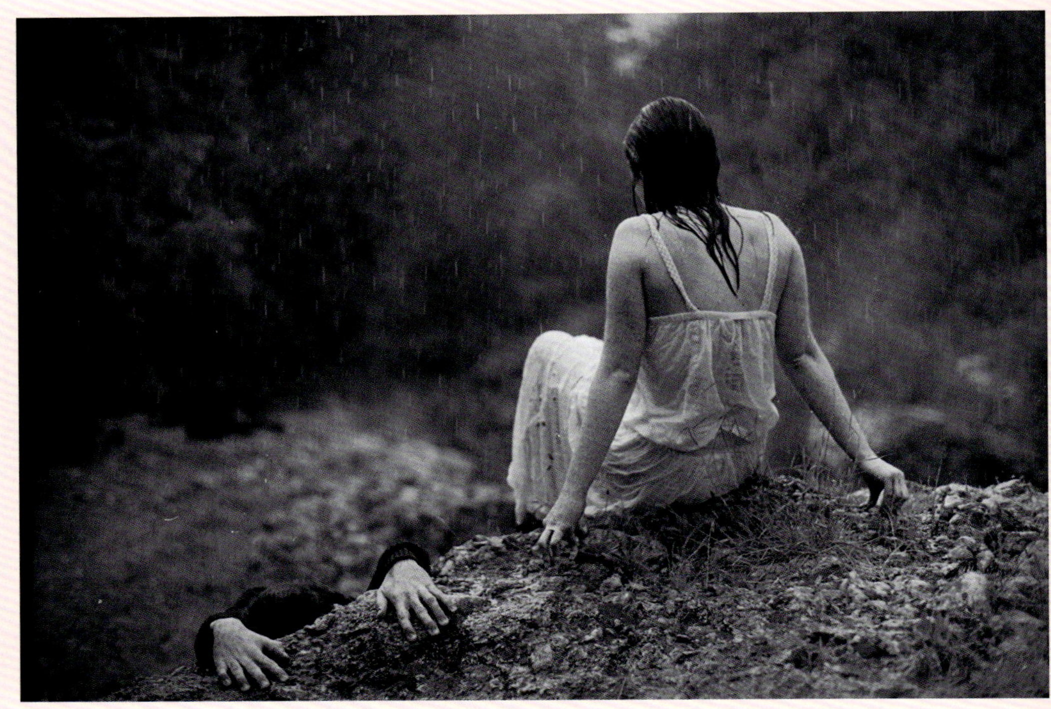

Hypnagogia #5, Andrea Torres Balaguer, 2013

DIRECTING EMOTION

GUIDING THE VIEWER'S FEELINGS

At first glance, a minimalist photograph can often appear to be lacking in complexity, yet it is this inherent simplicity that can communicate powerful emotions and create an intense and lasting connection with a viewer. Photographs with an emotive subject matter or thoughtful narrative can inspire curiosity and imagination in your audience, encouraging them to look deeper and question the significance of the elements they contain.

A powerful minimalist image can stop a viewer in their tracks and force them to think about what they are looking at. It leaves breathing space for interpretation and prompts emotional and psychological engagement.

As a minimalist photographer, you have the power to mould this visceral response by carefully planning your image. Think about the mood, tone and atmosphere you wish to capture, and choose a subject which helps to convey these elements clearly. By layering the scene with careful framing and thoughtful composition, you are helping to guide a viewer's journey through the photograph.

Ultimately, however, while the photographer can provide some parameters, each viewer will read these clues in a different way, based on their personal perceptions and past experiences. It is this immersive experience that will create a lasting impression in the viewer's mind.

Here, Andrea Torres Balaguer conveys mixed emotions through the placement and direction of the subjects in the frame. The woman in white is positioned slightly off-centre, suggesting feelings of anticipation, while her gaze across the scene invites the viewer to follow an implied path and question what she can see.[1] The visible hands of the mysterious second person create an immediate sense of ambiguity: they force us to ask uncomfortable questions and provide compelling visual tension. The viewer must explore the relationship between presence and absence.

Torres has, therefore, created a stripped back, but cryptic dialogue which has the power to lead each viewer to a different narrative. The emotional direction helps to shape our feelings by leading our focus and attention to elements that are and are not in the frame. It is up to us, however, to find the meaning that most resonates, which is often the one that is based upon our own memories and past experiences.

[1] *See* Lines and Pathways pp. 74–7

BLUR

SOFTEN LINES TO PLAY WITH MEANING

Blur has a varied role in minimalist photography. It can be introduced to help refine a composition by softening or obscuring background details or specific areas that may otherwise detract from the minimalist aesthetic. Used thoughtfully, blur can reveal just enough information to invite contemplation, without distracting from the subject. This can isolate the subject and draw attention to it, helping you create a cohesive and visually pleasing image that invites your audience to connect with the main elements in the scene.

From an artistic standpoint, blur can add a unique aesthetic to a minimalist photograph. Blurring an entire image will naturally remove definitive boundaries by softening lines, blending colours and creating an alternative visual interest to the composition. The image will be reduced to one of peacefulness and calm, creating a more immersive experience for the viewer.

Here, Uta Barth has used blur to reduce the scene to its essence. This conceptual image engages the audience by asking what it is they are looking at and perhaps what their expectations of a photograph should be. There is an absence of a traditional focal point or clearly defined subject, which encourages the viewer to interpret the scene for themselves, rather than relying on visual prompts or a given narrative.[1] This photograph – which may perhaps have been a relatively 'ordinary' or mundane scene – is transposed into something out of the ordinary.

Many cameras allow you to turn off or override autofocus. By deliberately defocusing the lens you can intentionally blur the entire image, which will create an ethereal soft-focus effect as seen in the image here.

Alternatively, blurring certain areas can affect the depth, layout and framing of the scene. The most common way to achieve this is by selectively focusing on one particular detail and letting the rest of the image fall out of focus. This is a powerful way to draw attention to a particular element if the remainder of the image is blurred.

Finally, a slow shutter speed combined with movement will create a blurred effect.[2] If the camera is intentionally moved while the shutter is open, it will create a blurred abstract effect. Similarly, if the subject or objects move and the camera remains stationary, these elements will be blurred while the remainder of the scene is captured correctly.

[1] *See* Focal Point pp. 28–9
[2] *See* Movement pp. 88–91

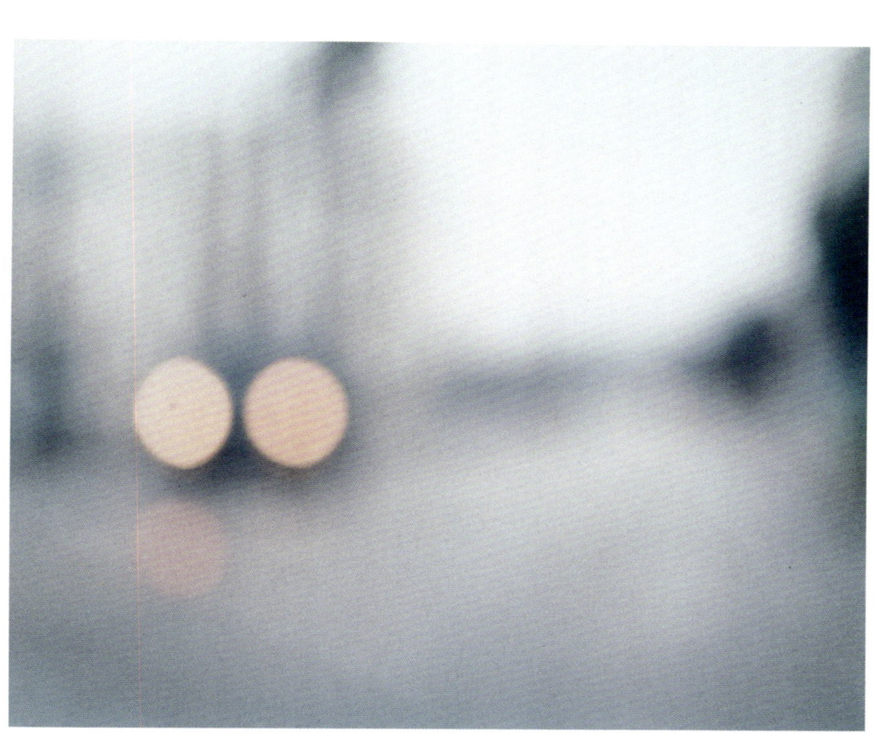

***Field #9*, Uta Barth, 1995**

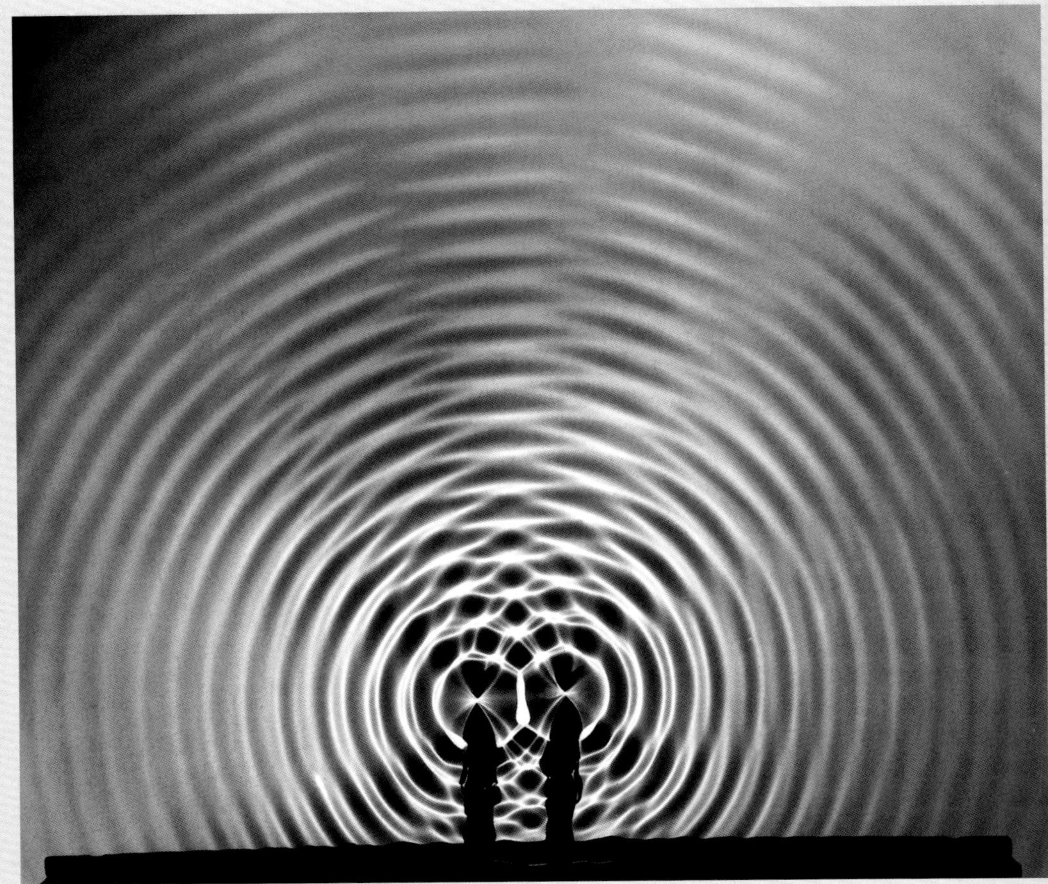

Interference Pattern, Berenice Abbott, 1958–61

FOCUS

USE FOCUS TO CREATE MOVEMENT

Focus is an essential feature that helps determine the impact and clarity of an element or area in a photograph. When incorporated precisely into a minimalist composition, the sharper areas will guide the viewer's perception, understanding and interpretation of their purpose.

Where the image is centred around a few key elements, such as the arrangement of lines, textures, colours or shapes, sharp focus can draw attention to the beauty found in their simplicity. This can invite viewers to appreciate the elegance and aesthetics of the minimal elements.

The mood, atmosphere and overall emotional tone of an image can be altered significantly by focus as well, so experiment with how much of your images you allow to appear 'sharp'. When your entire image is sharply focused it will convey a sense of clarity, precision and detail that can help to accentuate its simplicity. Ensuring that all details are sharp will help to convey a detailed story to an audience which can lead to a greater understanding and appreciation of the scene as they explore the entire image and details within.

Alternatively a softly focused image naturally suggests a more dreamy, relaxing and tranquil experience, where the partial lack of detail can prompt the viewers imagination and invite a more personal interpretation.

Selective focus can also help to enhance the visual interest of a minimalist image. This is where there is intentional focus placed on a specific part of the scene or single subject, drawing more attention to it by giving it more visual weight.[1] Depth of field control using a wide aperture setting (such as f/2.8) will result in a shallow depth of field and create a sharp subject with a blurred background.[2] This contrast will create a naturally pleasing balance between the sharpness of the subject and the softness of the background (or foreground).

In this mesmerizing image, Berenice Abbott captures an oscillating wave pattern in an almost abstract manner.[3] Our eyes are immediately drawn to the sharpest points in the image, which are positioned at the lower centre of the composition. The radiating circular patterns quickly fall out of focus and this transition from sharp to soft focus creates a sense of depth and movement. The viewer will naturally follow these patterns as the sharpness disappears and the focus fades away. The hypnotic reduction in clarity produces a meditative quality, while also capturing the essence and beauty that can be found in nature and scientific exploration.

[1] *See* Focal Point pp. 28–9
[2] *See* Blur pp. 94–5
[3] *See* Abstracts pp. 84–5

STORYTELLING

SOLITUDE AND ISOLATION

PLACE A SOLITARY SUBJECT IN AN UNCLUTTERED SCENE

Solitude and isolation are two incredibly powerful and evocative themes. When conveyed through minimalist photography, they have the ability to communicate intensely with the audience and provoke a deep emotional feeling.

Solitude generally implies a voluntary choice to be alone, where the subject is in a solitary location, or away from a busy environment. There is a positivity to this choice, which suggests a sense of freedom and empowerment. Successfully capturing this intimacy and the beauty of moments spent alone will influence the visual and emotional journey for the viewer.

In this image, the lone figure climbing the staircase immediately evokes a feeling of solitude. I made a deliberate choice to frame the composition so the emphasis was on the large surrounding emptiness. This creates a visual metaphor for the emotional distances and difficult journey the man faces, and the large area of negative space intensifies the sense of seclusion.[1] The choice of a muted colour palette adds to the emotional impact by emphasizing the simplicity of the scene and placing additional focus on the subject.[2]

You can use solitude in the context of minimalist photography to narrate visual stories of personal growth, vulnerability and introspection, and as a way of conveying the quiet and serene beauty in a scene. Both approaches invite the viewer to reflect on their own experiences of being alone.

Images focusing on the emotions associated with solitude and being alone can manifest in a variety of ways, both in terms of your composition and subject choices. Capturing fleeting moments of quiet and stillness in a busy environment, or generally empty or desolate spaces that are absent of human presence, are both ways in which you can emphasize the solitude of an environment.[3]

However, solitude does not always need to be portrayed as actual physical separation. It can also be represented on an emotional level, which you can suggest through specific expressions, body language or other implicit clues. Metaphors are also powerful tools you can employ to symbolize a solitary feeling; a single element out of place or away from its usual position or company, or an isolated item devoid of the human interaction usually associated with it are both valid approaches here.[4]

[1] *See* Negative Space pp. 18–9
[2] *See* Colour Palette pp. 52–5
[3] *See* Silence pp. 112–3
[4] *See* Symbolism and Metaphor pp. 124–5

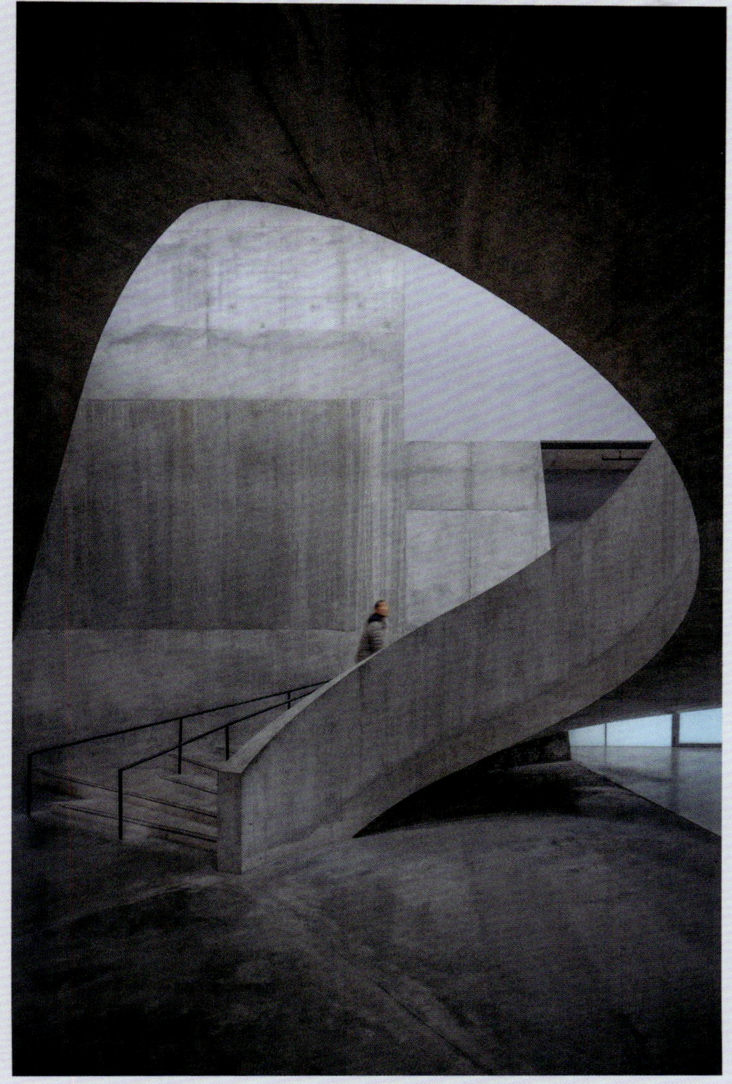

Rising up Alone, Antony Zacharias, 2022

Isolation and the resulting emotional detachment are powerful notions that can elicit deep connections with the audience, as they are often associated with a state of being alone, usually through a lack of choice or control. Because it is usually involuntary or unintentional – the result of external factors – the sense of feeling isolated can conjure up connotations of loneliness, alienation, disconnection and helplessness in the visual narrative.

Eiji Ohashi captures a wonderful feeling of isolation in the image opposite. The subject – a vending machine – is placed centrally in the composition, surrounded by a large expanse of desolate snowy landscape. This unexpected location amplifies the sense of isolation as the viewer is drawn into the emptiness and quiet that surrounds the subject. The fading light of dusk creates a sombre ambiance that adds to these feelings.

It is also symbolic that there is no human presence in the image. Vending machines are designed to interact with people and are usually placed in busy locations, but this photograph highlights its seclusion and invites the audience to contemplate their own feelings of loneliness and detachment.

Generally, including vast areas that are devoid of detail will accentuate the emptiness in your images and help distance them from the busy, complex environments we are more accustomed to. Placing your focus on a solitary subject within such a setting can effectively convey a sense of vulnerability, whereby the subject evokes empathy and a deeper connection to the viewer. Limiting the amount of detail and other distracting elements in your composition will provide fewer visual cues for the viewer, which prompts them to fill in any narrative gaps themselves. This actively amplifies their engagement with the image, as they are left to draw from memories and personal experience.

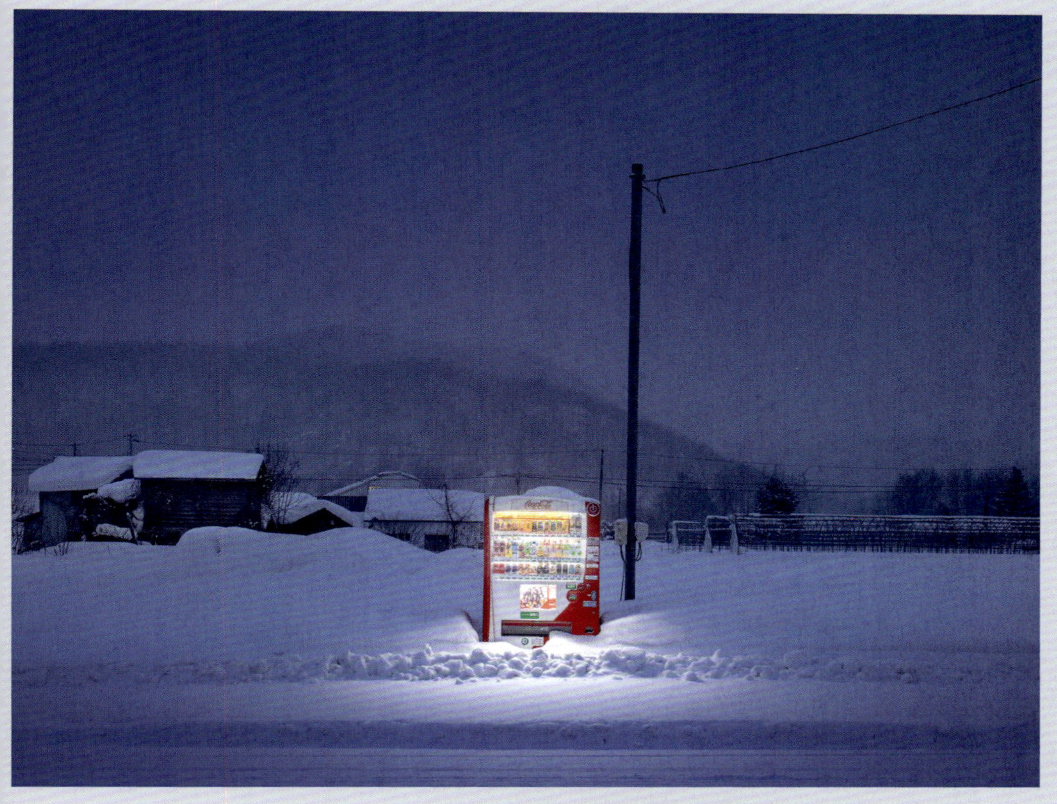

Roadside Lights #139 (Setose, Hokkaido), Eiji Ohashi, 2021

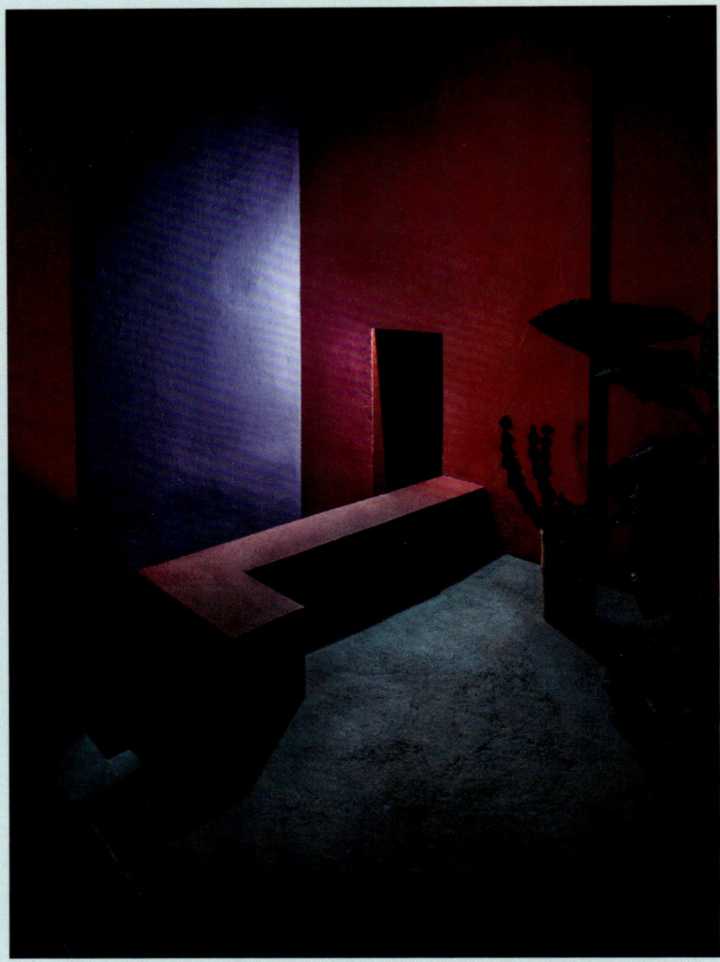

Cactus, Antony Zacharias, 2022

NIGHT PHOTOGRAPHY

CREATE A CINEMATIC SCENE AFTER DARK

Minimalist photographs taken at night have a look that is very different to those taken during the day. Many scenes are transformed after the sun has set, resulting in stronger images that are simultaneously sombre and evocative. Reduced visibility, the play of light and shadow, and the appearance of artificial lights all provide opportunities to create incredibly striking minimalist images.[1]

The lighting is key when you are capturing images at night. Artificial lights will illuminate only a limited area, and this will affect how certain elements are revealed in the scene – if they are revealed at all. Meanwhile, the areas of darkness will hide large sections that can help maintain simplicity in your composition.

Direct, bright light sources will create strong shadows and vivid highlights. As they appear more dramatic in the frame, these bright areas naturally have more visual weight and significance.[2] Conversely, the illumination from softer, diffused lights will change the overall mood of the image, with a gentler contrast and gradual transition between light and shadow.[3] This more delicate lighting will ensure that the illuminated area remains visible, but without overpowering your composition. It will contribute to a feeling of calm and serenity, and often produces a dreamlike quality that envelops your subject in a subtle glow. This can enhance the emotional undertones of an image without overpowering or distracting from the simplicity of your composition.

As well as paying attention to the quality of the light, you should also think about the colour of the available lighting, as this also impacts on the overall look and feel of an image. Warmer orange and yellow hues, and cooler tones from bluer light sources, will alter the atmosphere of your scene in very different ways.

[1] *See* Shadows and Highlights pp. 46–7
[2] *See* Balance and Visual Weight pp. 14–5
[3] *See* Contrast pp. 44–5

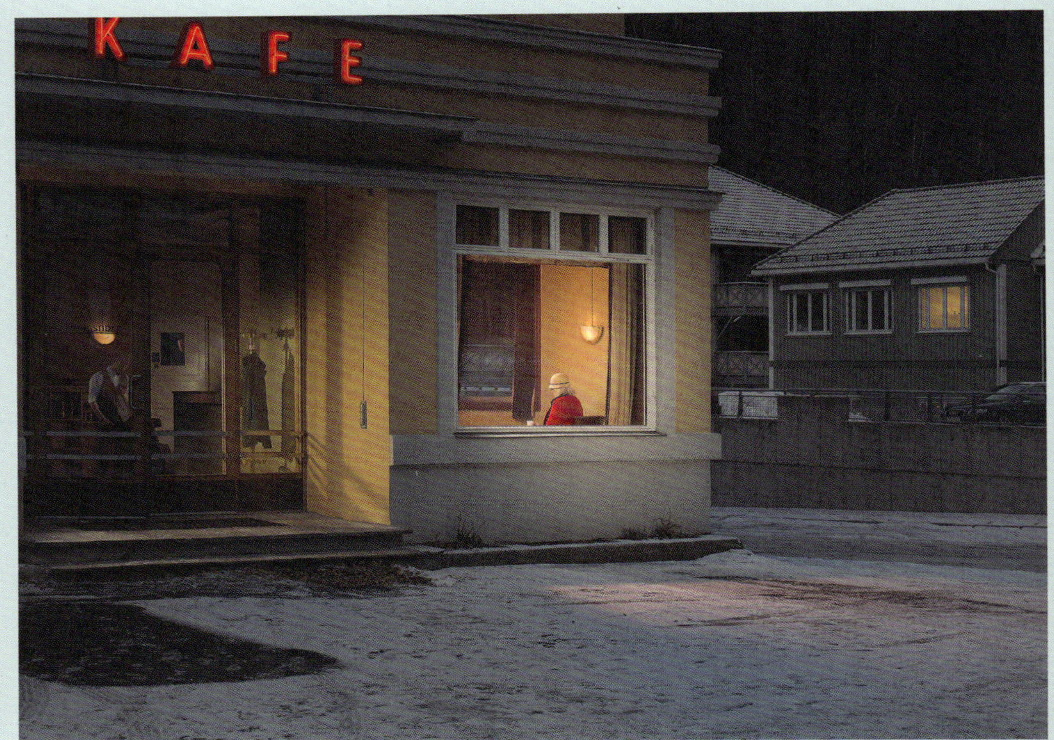

Slow Night, Ole Marius Joergensen, 2019

In the image on page 104, which was taken late in the night, the colours are dramatically different to their daytime appearance.[4] There is still a vibrancy to the scene, but it is more diluted than it is in bright daylight. The strong, dark shadows play a more prominent role, with their long and angular shapes adding graphic elements to the scene. They help introduce a sense of mystery that is highly conducive to minimalist photographs.[5] These pronounced shadows also help transform more mundane objects – such as the cactus – into captivating silhouettes, while the artificial lights cast an eerie glow that partially illuminates the architecture that is just out of view.[6] This unique interaction between light and darkness helps to turn the image into something evocative that invites the viewer to explore it further.

By comparison, Ole Marius Joergensen's image embodies the essence of minimalism through his use of composition and lighting. Placing focus on a lone figure visible through a café window conveys a real sense of solitude and introspection that draws the audience into the quiet moment. The nocturnal setting plays a crucial role in enhancing the nature of the image, lending it an atmosphere of tranquillity that invites contemplation by the viewer.

The composition is deliberately sparse, with unnecessary details falling into soft shadow. Although centrally positioned, the subject and the window are surrounded by negative space, which is darkened by the night.[7] This helps to accentuate the figure and emphasizes their significance in the simple composition.

Generally, there is an inherent silence at night that will play a significant role in your minimalist images. Night scenes are usually devoid of crowds and other regular daytime activities, which can help create cleaner compositions, so think about revisiting popular locations after dark to see how the atmosphere changes. The mood set by the available lighting will directly affect the way your story or intended emotion is conveyed to the audience, but remember that balance and simplicity remain integral to the creation of interesting images – you still need to pay attention to the impact of each element in your composition.

[4] *See* Colour Palette pp. 52–5
[5] *See* Mystery pp. 128–9
[6] *See* Silhouette pp. 48–9
[7] *See* Negative Space pp. 18–9

ELEVATING THE MUNDANE

SPOTLIGHT THE EVERYDAY

At first glance, this stark view of a living room by William Eggleston may seem mundane, but look deeper and it offers a more complex story. This photograph captures the nostalgia and essence of an ordinary moment in a time gone by, but is free from too many distracting elements. Despite its sparse appearance (or perhaps because of it) the limited number of objects – the chairs, organ and small gilded frame on the large wall – encourage the viewer to imagine the home's occupants and the room being more 'alive'.

You may feel as if there are limited opportunities to create interesting photographs close to home, and that you have to travel to distant shores to capture something spectacular. However, in reality, wonderful minimalist images can be found all around you. Often, all you need to do is slow down, appreciate where you are and be aware of what surrounds you.

A compelling minimalist image – that is, one to which your audience will connect in both a visual and emotional way – need not be a grandiose subject or scene. There doesn't always have to be a complex meaning or direct message. Indeed, there is something to be said for the charm that exists in the smaller, more 'everyday' items that surround us, and documenting your immediate surroundings in your daily life can lead to images that are full of beauty and significance. The intimate narratives and insights into your personal world will likely resonate with your audience, prompting their own memories, stories or perhaps even a feeling of nostalgia.

The simple fact is that what may be insignificant to you can be 'foreign' to someone else. Adopting a sense of mindfulness will help here, so slow down or stop to look and appreciate your current surroundings. Think about potential subjects and what they mean to you: how do they make you feel and why do you want to include them in your image?

The ability to capture seemingly banal views in your minimalist photographs offers valuable insights into your personal experiences, and the opportunity to preserve these in an image you can share. This, in turn, can create a strong emotional tie with your audience.

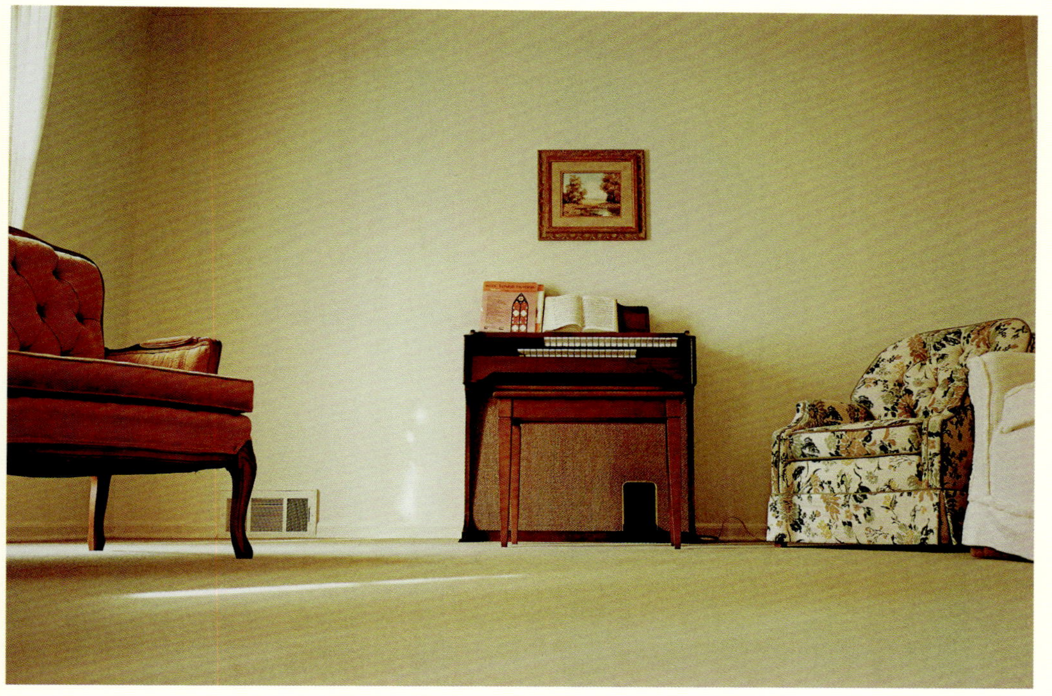

Untitled (Plate 11 of 15 from the Troubled Waters Portfolio), William Eggleston, 1980

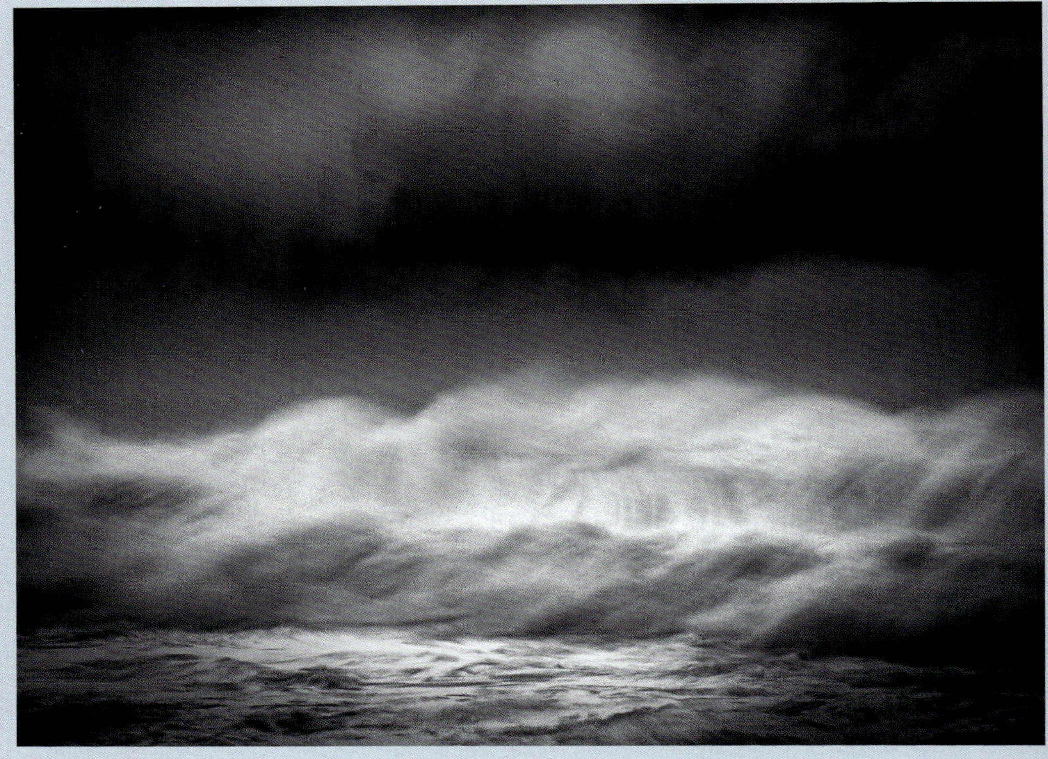

The Storm, Antony Zacharias, 2021

NATURE AND ATMOSPHERE

DISTIL NATURAL SCENES TO THEIR KEY ELEMENTS

The inherent beauty found in nature can create visually arresting photographs, especially when it is conveyed in a straightforward and elegant way. Consequently, minimalist photographs that focus on the natural world will often lead to aesthetically pleasing images.

From a minimalist perspective, using simplicity to communicate the essence of nature will resonate with your viewer. Reducing a scene to a few key elements will encourage your audience to appreciate subtleties that may otherwise be overlooked in a more complex composition. Basic shapes, forms, patterns and textures will all become more pronounced, and your viewers will be invited to slow down and become more mindful as they contemplate the intimate details within the frame.

When setting out to capture the photograph shown here, I was mesmerized by the power and ferocity of the storm and the ocean. The relentless energy of the violent waves immediately sets the tone for the narrative, and the minimalist composition focuses only on what is essential and the feelings conveyed. It is an immediate and impactful experience, and the viewer can engage fully with the unfolding drama without distraction. To help tell the story I used a slightly longer exposure to add an energetic blur and strong sense of movement to the crashing waves, which emphasizes the raw power, mood and scale of the storm.[1]

Although my image depicts the essence of a ferocious storm, many natural world minimalist images present a sense of peace and serenity. A single element – or a few simple elements – can evoke feelings of tranquillity that allow the viewer to relax and wander through the scene, free of confusion or distraction.[2] Look for larger areas of sky, water or other natural features that can serve as a visual respite, as well as providing balance to the elements contained within. This can also be an effective way to suggest a sense of scale and create a scene that is spacious and open;[3] one that will foster a deeper connection with the viewer. Using negative space can play an important part in this, and you can use it to emphasize the subject and frame it within your composition.[4]

Finally, consider using monochrome, muted tones or a limited colour palette, as each of these can contribute to the minimalist aesthetic. Contrast and tone can also help to add depth and focus to the image, especially when it comes to drawing attention to the main focal point(s).

[1] *See* Long Exposure pp. 86–7
[2] *See* Tranquillity pp. 116–7
[3] *See* Scale pp. 20–1
[4] *See* Negative Space pp. 18–9

SILENCE

PARE BACK TO CREATE A VISUALLY QUIET SCENE

There is an inherent stillness within this image, which seemingly exudes silence. The audience is invited to experience this meditative and contemplative space; to reflect on the quiet simplicity before them. The minimalist composition of the rocks (representing stability) and the floating, transient branch all contribute to the overall sense of calm. For this image, captured early on a misty morning, the longer exposure time has removed any visible movement or ripples from the water.[1]

Silence in minimalist photography goes beyond the absence of audible noise or distraction. It is an artistic expression of calm and stillness, where any discernible noise from the outside world vanishes and the beauty in the image is left to speak for itself.

Creating silence in an image requires some initial planning and thought. For a start, you need to ask yourself what is going to be the main focal point. What will the foundation of your contemplative image be? Where will you position the various elements in the frame, and how will your placement promote feelings of silence that will resonate with your audience? This is all about stripping a scene back to its basics – the 'essence' of what you want to show. It is about seeking out simple compositions, subdued colours and shapes, and carefully balancing the elements in the frame so they reveal intrinsic beauty without any distraction.

Clean lines, symmetry and stability can all contribute to a feeling of silence, but they need to evoke a visual harmony within the image; a form of stillness similar to the intoxicating quiet we can find in nature and remote environments. The viewer should have the time and space in your image to contemplate the scene and make sense of the elements.

As a general rule, you should avoid bright, saturated colours, as these can be overly stimulating for a 'quiet' image, and instead seek out muted tones in the form of pastel or neutral colour palettes.[2] Alternatively, a monochrome treatment can emphasize shape, form and structure, without the distraction of colour.

Light will also play an important role in shaping the atmosphere and mood of your images. Softly diffused light will contribute to a calming atmosphere, allowing subtle details to be revealed without strong, distracting contrasts. Indeed, soft shadows, low contrast and a delicate tonal gradation can all be significant when it comes to shaping stillness and mood.

[1] *See* Long Exposure pp. 86–7
[2] *See* Colour Palette pp. 52–5

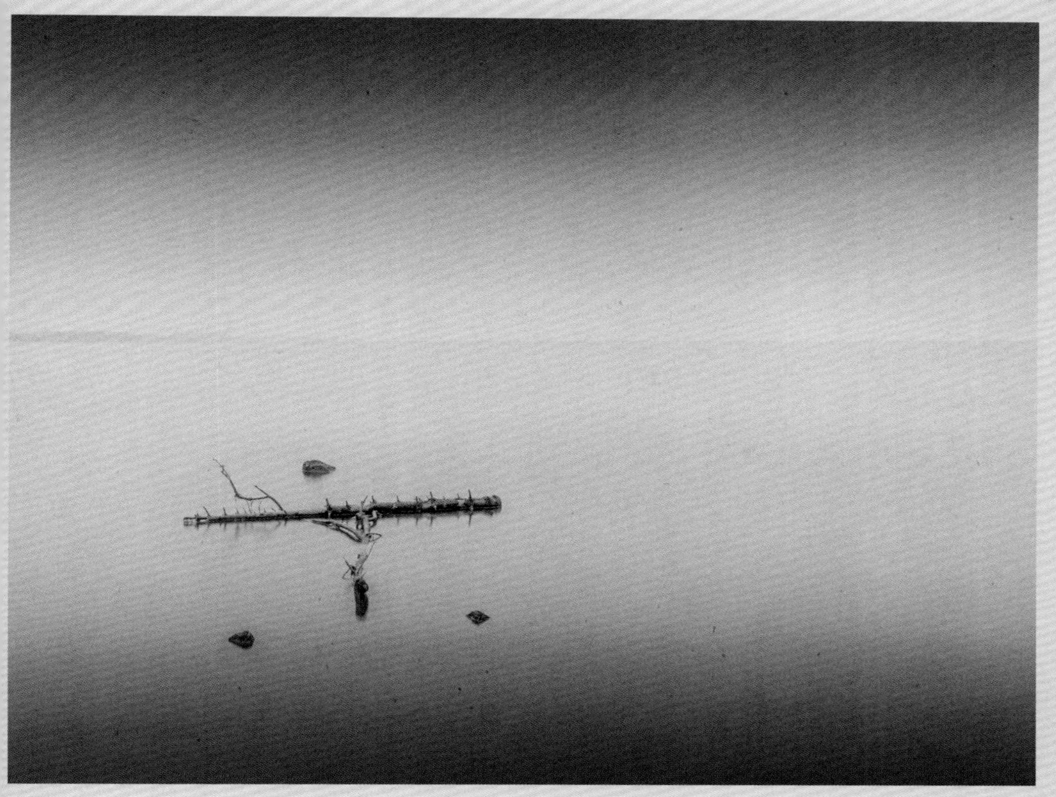

Afloat, Antony Zacharias, 2019

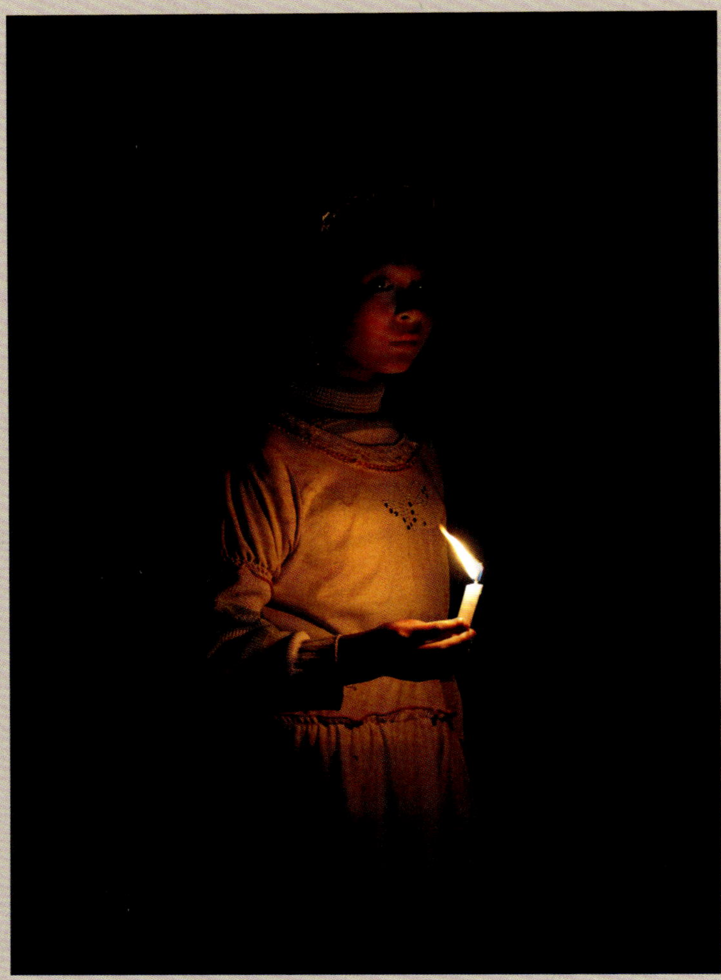

Absorbed, Shauneen Kelly, 2014

SUBTLE GESTURES

PHOTOGRAPH SOMEONE WITH EXPRESSION

The minimalist approach to photography and simplicity focuses the viewer's attention on the essence and importance of a subject.

An effective minimalist portrait lies in its ability to connect with the viewer, evoke emotion and tell a story.[1] There is a real opportunity to go beyond an image that simply shows 'the subject', and this is something you can achieve by incorporating their subtle expressions into the photograph. These small gestures can infuse a portrait with emotion and character, which will naturally help to convey the subject's mood or personality. However, it can be challenging to anticipate and capture these fleeting moments, particularly as you don't want to overwhelm the minimalist aesthetic and the natural simplicity of the composition.

Shauneen Kelly's portrait is more than just a visual representation of a young girl: it is an intimate image that is full of emotion and feeling. The minimalist composition focuses on the subtleties of the child illuminated by candlelight. The negative space[2] isolates her in the frame, enabling the viewer to focus on her intense gaze and apparent concentration, which highlight her dedication to the ceremony she is involved in. The soft, diffused light adds depth to the composition and draws further attention to the subject, while strong shadow areas hide distracting elements in the background.

By excluding any superfluous elements, the viewer is immediately connected with the subject. They are drawn into a direct, almost personal interaction with the individual, and are invited to decipher the nuanced language of the subject's body language and interpret the unspoken emotions hidden within the frame. This interactive aspect of photography engages the viewer in an intense way, encouraging contemplation and fostering a profound connection between the subject and themselves.

The technical aspects of a minimalist portrait will naturally play a crucial role. The lighting, composition, colour (vibrant, subdued or even none) and contrast are all elements you need to consider: each have an impact on the mood of your portrait. This type of image is still open to experimentation and creativity, though. Different techniques and perspectives will change the way that gestures and expressions are captured, and emotions are conveyed. They will influence the visual appeal of the image and ultimately how the viewer connects with the subject.

[1] *See* Portraits pp. 26–7
[2] *See* Negative Space pp. 18–9

SLOW DOWN TO CREATE CONNECTION

Tranquillity and mindfulness are two underlying concepts in minimalist photography that together help unify an image and create a meditative space where the audience can pause and reflect.

Mindfulness is the consideration and conscious attention that we give to the present moment. In minimalist photography this extends beyond technical skills and equipment and is the mindset you need to create an engaging image. It requires you as a photographer to be present in the moment and immersed in the entire process of capturing your photograph – from the initial concept, through composition and lighting, to the narrative and feelings that you want to convey.

At each stage, being mindful will help you nurture a deeper connection with your subject and the final image. You can achieve part of this by slowing down and observing, paying careful attention to the details and nuances that may otherwise be easily overlooked, and making conscious and considered choices about what to include and what to leave out of your photograph. Ask yourself how the individual elements help to unify the composition and successfully communicate your message. Patience, focus and clarity are all central to mindfulness and the creation of images that will resonate with the viewer.

Tranquillity in a minimalist photograph refers to the feelings of calm and serenity that the audience feels when they are looking at an elegant composition that has been stripped back to a few key elements, framed with a sense of order, clarity and harmony. This is something that you can achieve when an image exudes quiet and invites contemplation;[1] when a strong emotional connection is formed between the subject and the audience, despite the photograph's overwhelming simplicity.

Negative space and visual balance are two of the creative tools you can call on to help convey feelings of tranquillity in an image. Together they can suggest a sense of freedom that invites your viewer to appreciate the subject, while simultaneously providing quiet simplicity in the surrounding emptiness.[2]

Hengki Koentjoro's image immediately evokes a sense of a calm. It is a contemplative space in which viewers can immerse themselves. Free from the potential distractions of vibrant colours, each layer – the still water, lone temple and distant mountains fading into a delicate gradient of cloud and mist – adds to the serene atmosphere, encouraging a moment of reflection and inner peace, free from the distractions of urban environments.

[1] *See* Simplicity pp. 12–3
[2] *See* Silence pp. 112–3

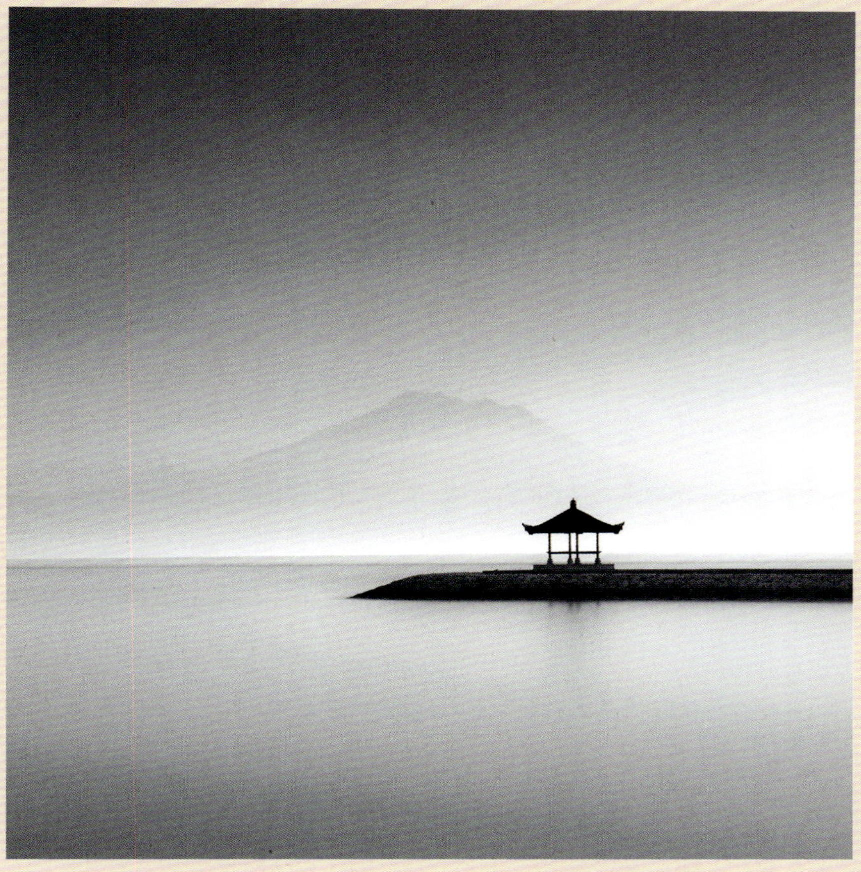

MN04, Hengki Koentjoro, 2014

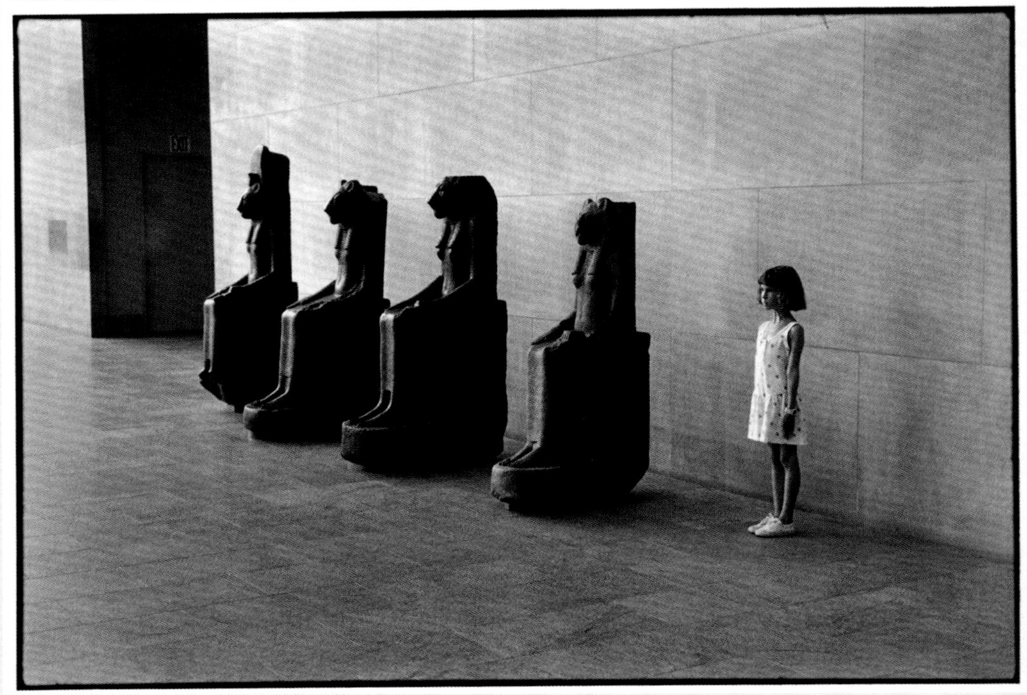

The Metropolitan Museum of Art, New York City, Elliott Erwitt, 1988

JUXTAPOSITION

HIGHLIGHT DIFFERENCES TO ADD A SENSE OF PLAY

With this simple, yet captivating composition, Elliott Erwitt has created a playful minimalist image. The young girl is aligned with four ancient statues in a museum, which leads the viewer to make a direct comparison between their contrasting characteristics – the modern and the ancient – and reflect on the passage of time.[1] The simplicity of contrasting the young girl with the grandeur of her surroundings creates a powerful and engaging image, which illustrates how carefully juxtaposed elements in a minimalist photograph can convey deeper meaning and emotion.

Juxtaposition refers to the deliberate placement of two or more elements in the frame in such a way that it highlights their differences, creating or strengthening the photograph's message. These elements (whether they are actual objects or mere concepts) and the way they are compared will increase the visual interest of a photograph. This can be a powerful technique when it comes to the creation of striking and impactful minimalist images, where the simplicity of the composition will emphasize the juxtaposed elements.[2]

Usually, juxtaposed elements are read together to help tell a story.[3] There are numerous ways in which you can use contrasting elements to convey a message, evoke an emotion or emphasize differences or similarities. Using juxtaposition effectively requires you to pay attention to your subject, detail and composition. It is vital that you consider the placement of elements throughout the frame, to ensure that the contrast between them is both intentional and impactful. Explore different camera angles, distances and lighting to find the strongest composition and balance for your juxtaposed elements.

Of course, effective juxtaposition is not limited to obvious visual comparisons. You can also contrast symbolic elements, colour, tone, texture, movement or even silence and implied sound – any one of these can be used to great creative effect. Presenting subtle comparisons can encourage your viewers to engage with your images, as our minds are naturally predisposed to decipher subtle messages.[4] However, it is important not to overwhelm the audience by including too many contrasting details. The aim is to create a subtle, yet clear and compelling contrast between key elements that convey a message or emotion while enhancing the impact of the image.

[1] *See* Symbolism and Metaphor pp. 124–5
[2] *See* Simplicity pp. 12–3
[3] *See* Narrative in Composition pp. 130–3
[4] *See* Curiosity pp. 122–3

TENSION

SURROUND A SUBJECT IN DARKNESS TO CREATE SUSPENSE

Yasuhiro Ogawa's photograph *Autumn Bridge* immediately presents the viewer with a feeling of suspense and foreboding. The scene is devoid of much detail or obvious narrative, and the strong leading lines of the walkway guide us into the darkness that abounds. Only a few branches of a tree with leaves in bright fiery colours appear mysteriously visible and seize attention. While a muted colour palette is often a common feature of minimalist photography, here a single element with striking colours helps to add to the feeling of anxiety and uneasiness.[1]

There are times when you can look at scene in front of you and immediately feel a sense of anticipation, anxiety or possibly discomfort. The way that certain elements seemingly interact may evoke feelings of potential conflict and tension.[2] Conveying these emotions in a minimalist image can lead to incredibly powerful and impactful images that invite the viewer to delve deeper. Whether the feelings are subtle or more pronounced, much of the narrative is left to the viewer's imagination, which creates a wonderfully immersive experience.

In a minimalist photograph, where the essence of a scene is simplified and stripped back, introducing tension can add a layer of emotional depth. The idea of reducing unnecessary elements and placing emphasis on those that remain, provides an opportunity to evoke quite intense feelings. Tension can create anything from a moderate sense of excitement and anticipation, through to significant discomfort and a sense of uneasiness. This additional layer of drama and energy helps an audience explore the image and engage with it in a unique way.

To start with, consider your choice of subjects and their placement in the frame, as this will have a fundamental impact on the tension you generate. Compositional techniques can be employed to create a powerful visual journey that guides the audience across the image, with areas of obvious unease helping to provide a sense of movement that directs the viewer to explore further.[3] Creating a sense of imbalance by breaking a repeating pattern or symmetry, or merely placing an element off-centre, can be enough to introduce discomfort and an anxious energy to an otherwise straightforward scene.[4] This can make your audience feel slight uncertainty, adding tension without overcomplicating your composition or detracting from the minimal aesthetic.

[1] *See* Colour Palette pp. 52–5
[2] *See* Visual Discord pp. 126–7
[3] *See* Lines and Pathways pp. 74–7
[4] *See* Symmetry and Asymmetry pp. 70–3

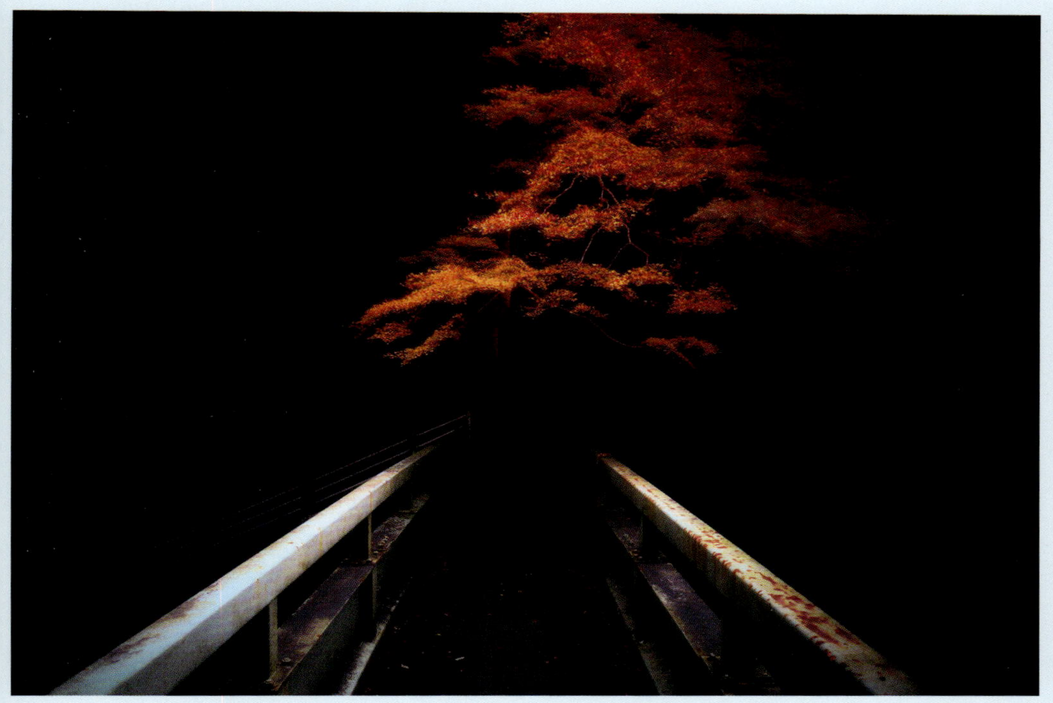

Autumn Bridge, from *Lost in Kyoto*, Yasuhiro Ogawa, 2014

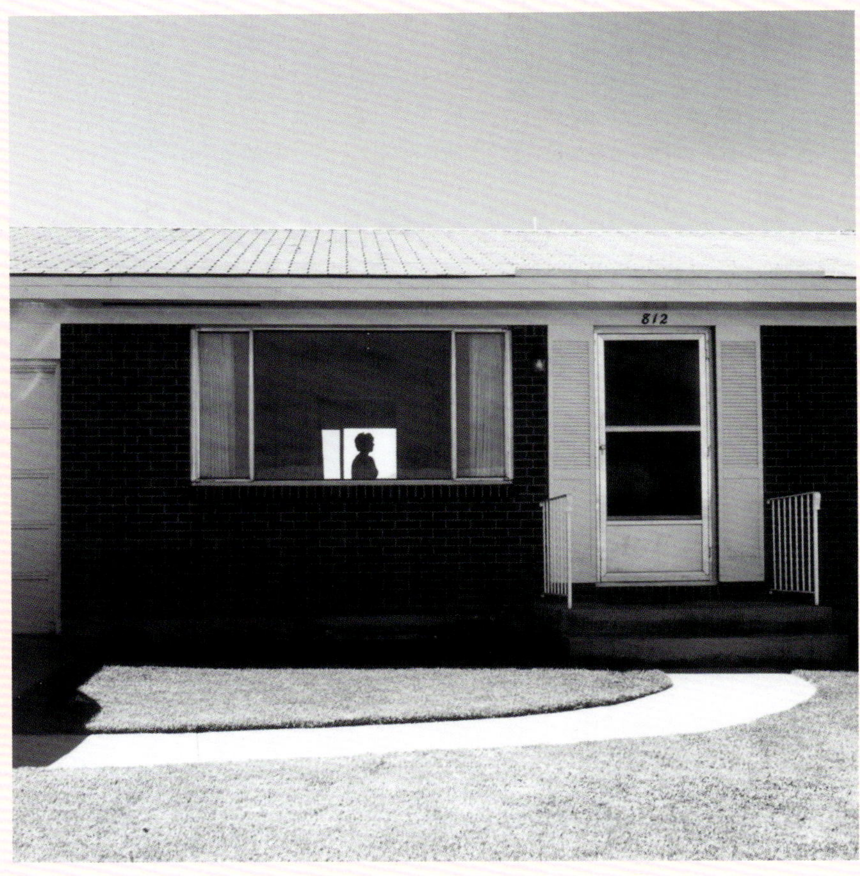

Colorado Springs, Robert Adams, 1968–70

CURIOSITY

SUGGEST MORE THAN YOU REVEAL

Inspiring curiosity in a minimalist photograph will help captivate an audience as they seek to interpret your image; the human mind is naturally inquisitive and enjoys trying to find meaning and understanding. Curiosity ties in directly with minimalist photography, as the restraint and simplicity in a composition can infer complex narratives, rather than presenting them outright. A lack of information or detail naturally leaves a lot of room for interpretation, especially compared to other types of photography where the message is clearly defined.[1] This invites the audience to use their imagination to complete the story, and because they are drawing on their own feelings and experiences while interacting with the image, it becomes more personal.

Robert Adams' compelling image *Colorado Springs* instantly evokes feelings of curiosity in the viewer. The use of shadows and light draw attention towards the central window and the silhouetted figure inside the building.[2] The notion of 'looking in' creates a unique dynamic that influences how the viewer connects with the image. The perfect positioning of the subject raises our curiosity and there is a natural desire to decipher and understand the story that is being revealed.

However, while a mixture of emotions are evoked by the image, these are largely determined subjectively by the viewer. Some people may feel a sense of calm or solitude surrounds the image, while others may feel a sense of mystery, apprehension and unease. These emotions are heightened by the simple minimalist composition, which encourages the viewer to create their own narrative based on the vague, yet compelling elements in the frame.

The absence of any obvious narrative or context in a minimalist image will naturally evoke curiosity. But you can also include subtle suggestions that will tempt the viewer to look harder and think more if they want to understand what they are looking at. Accordingly, you need to consider what you choose to photograph and how you frame your composition – the aim is to leave just enough clues to pique the interest of your audience so they want to look further.[3]

Minimalist compositions that suggest more than they reveal will inevitably lead to more memorable images. The viewer will not just look at the image, but actively explore it, seeking to understand it. In doing so, the audience will engage on a deeper level and the strong emotional connections they make will create a lasting impression.

[1] *See* Context pp. 134–5
[2] *See* Silhouette pp. 48–9
[3] *See* Narrative in Composition pp. 130–3

SYMBOLISM AND METAPHOR

USE AN ELEMENT TO CONVEY AN IDEA OR THEME

For generations art has included aspects of symbolism and metaphor as a means of communication. We can utilize these as photographers to influence how our audience relates to our work, as they navigate the significance of what has been included and sometimes omitted.

Symbolism is simply the use of certain elements within a composition to represent themes or ideas. These elements invite your audience to look beyond the literal image and gain a deeper insight into what you, as the photographer, are trying to say. While some symbolic elements and their placement will be obvious, others may not be so immediately apparent, making this is a powerful way to convey a message and create a connection with your viewer.

A metaphor is an implied message or theme, rather than a literal representation, and in a minimalist photograph it will be communicated by the way in which the elements or objects in the frame are connected or conveyed. Including just a few key elements and thinking about how they relate to one another can help guide the visual story you are telling. However, the viewer's interpretation of your images is subjective, so their response may vary; each individual will be led by their own emotions and experiences.

As a minimalist photographer, you need to consider how you can creatively use these techniques to establish a simple, yet clear visual narrative. Bear in mind that the elements don't have to be physical elements in the scene, but can also be created through your use of light, shadow, contrast and colour.

In this image, the illuminated doorway casts a fading light that serves as a subtle signpost to the viewer, drawing them into the brightness. The darkness and shadows appear haunting and perhaps suggest an intimidating place or a possible journey to overcome;[1] doorways are common metaphors for change, opportunity and transition. Here we can't see quite what is around the corner, which again invites us to think about where the different directions may lead us.[2]

The way that you choose to use symbolism or metaphors can help you go beyond presenting a straightforward message and enable you to start creating strong connections that will really make your audience think. If you can invite your viewers to look past what they are seeing initially and focus more on the 'why?' of your image, you can provoke a stronger emotional response that invites deeper thought and reflection in your minimalist photography.

[1] *See* Shadows and Highlights pp. 46–7
[2] *See* Mystery pp. 128–9

Red II, Antony Zacharias, 2022

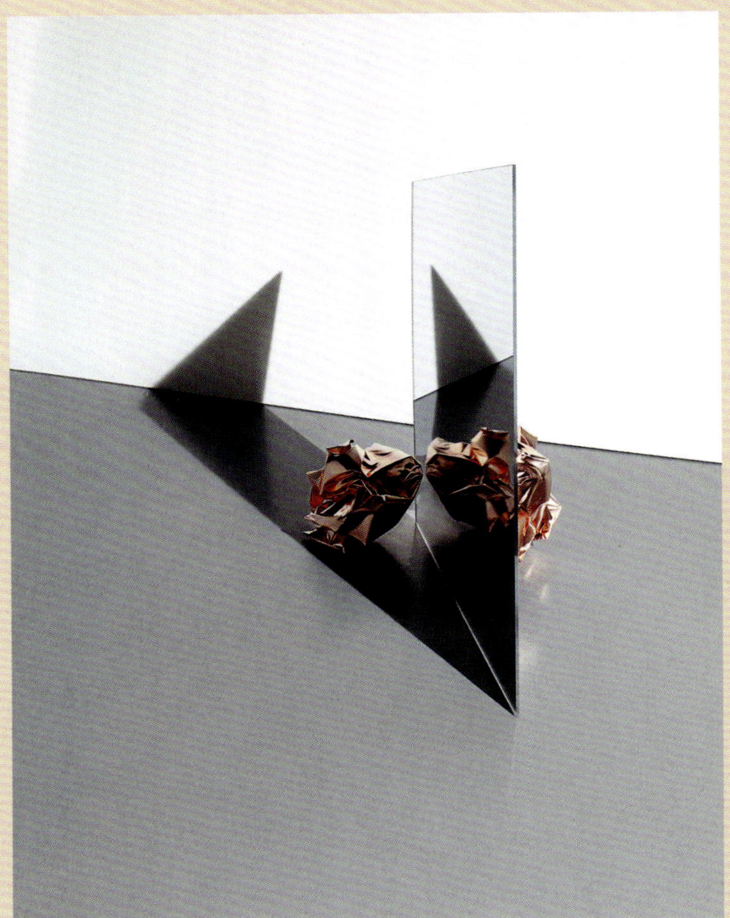

Becoming Aware, Beate Sonnenberg and Johanne Mills, 2016

VISUAL DISCORD

CHALLENGE WITH UNUSUAL OBJECTS AND ANGLES

There is a strong feeling of discord created in this image by Beate Sonnenberg and Johanne Mills. The disharmony between the shapes, colours and perceived textures of the elements is immediately evident. The mirror and reflections add depth, but also a sense of confusion to the composition. The position of the abstract objects is not as straightforward as it would initially seem,[1] and the pronounced angular shadows and tilted horizon add to the overall feeling of friction and contention.

The result is that the natural compositional balance is disrupted enough to provoke a feeling of disorder in what would be the norm. This engages the viewer, as they seek to understand what they are looking at and the significance of the elements throughout.

Visual discord in the context of minimalist photography refers to images that immediately provoke feelings of apprehension, disharmony and discomfort. Breaking the conventional rules of composition and introducing seemingly conflicting elements, or something that feels out of place, can create a powerful and thought-provoking image.

It may initially seem counter-intuitive and compositionally wrong to include clashing elements in a minimalist photograph, but introducing visual discord can lead to a more complex image that is more engaging and dynamic than one that is more straightforward. This is primarily because combining unsettling components introduces an element of surprise. It can challenge the viewer's expectations and invite them to question their understanding.

When you want to implement visual discord in a minimalist photograph, think about the interacting elements and how they might clash when they are placed together. The friction and discomfort between them shouldn't always be obvious and in a minimalist image it is vital that it is not overwhelming. Look at the involvement of elements with differing textures, shapes and contrast, and how light and shadow affect the image and its components. Creating a juxtaposition between opposing objects or symbols, or disrupting the natural or usual order will immediately result in a disturbed, tense composition.[2]

How you choose to capture your image can also create visual discord. Photographing from an unconventional perspective or angle will naturally disrupt how your viewers see the scene. Perhaps the easiest approach here is to replace the most widely used and familiar shooting angle – an eye-level view – with a significantly lower or higher camera angle. Either one can have a profound effect on the overall look and feel of your image.

[1] *See* Abstracts pp. 84–5
[2] *See* Tension pp. 120–1

MYSTERY

USE LIGHT AND SHADOW TO CREATE INTRIGUE

The power of mystery in a minimalist image lies in its ability to engage the viewer's imagination. It is about the power of suggestion and implication in a narrative that is only partially revealed. The human mind is naturally drawn to feelings of anticipation, so the invitation to try and interpret something thought-provoking is guaranteed to provide the viewer with a visually immersive experience.

Composition is crucial in evoking a sense of mystery, as it is the thoughtful arrangement of the elements in the frame that will help suggest a narrative and control your viewers' journey.[1] The strategic placement of subjects, careful framing and the use of negative space are all effective ways in which you can build intrigue.

Lighting is another critical aspect, as you can see in this image. Ray Metzker immediately draws the viewer into a powerful, ambiguous story, where the interplay of light, shadow and silhouette creates a mysterious atmosphere.[2] The elongated shadows hide just enough detail to prompt our imagination to fill in the details, while the long shafts of light reveal just enough to provoke interest. There is a wonderful combination of uncertainty and information, and a strong sense of trepidation and mystery that culminates with the two solitary backlit figures at the top of the stairs.[3]

There is a compelling cinematic feel to this scene, with the photographer capturing the wonderful grittiness of an urban environment. Photographs of cities can provide an opportunity to create drama and mystery through depth and space, underpinned by the complex stories of the buildings, streets and people that exist within it. Fleeting moments and partial narratives can transport viewers into the scene and hint at larger, more mysterious stories that continue to develop after the photograph is taken.

Creating a sense of mystery requires you to choose your subject with care. A simple subject – perhaps one that is isolated, partially revealed or even a little abstract and unclear – can become a powerful focal point. In a minimalist context this will inevitably engage the viewer's curiosity and encourage them to explore further. However, simplicity doesn't have to equate to the absence of content or limit narrative; it is the ability to use a few key elements with restraint, so you direct the viewer's imagination with more precision.[4]

[1] *See* Narrative in Composition pp. 130–3
[2] *See* Shadows and Highlights pp. 46–7
[3] *See* Mystery pp. 128–9
[4] *See* Simplicity pp. 12–3

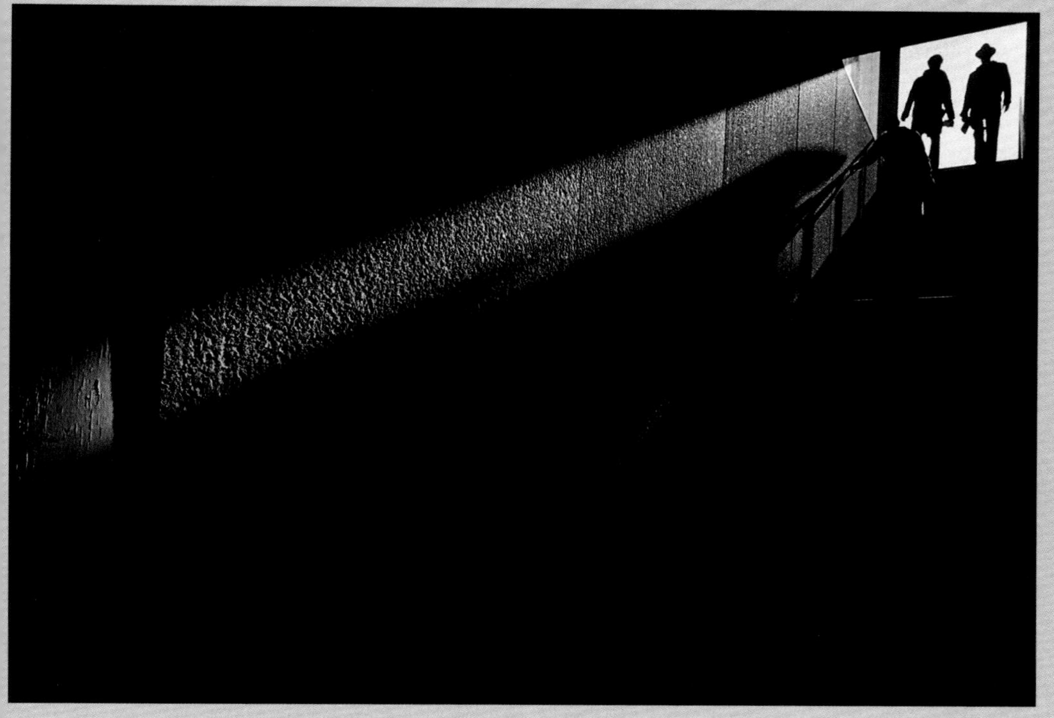

City Whispers, Ray Metzker, 1981

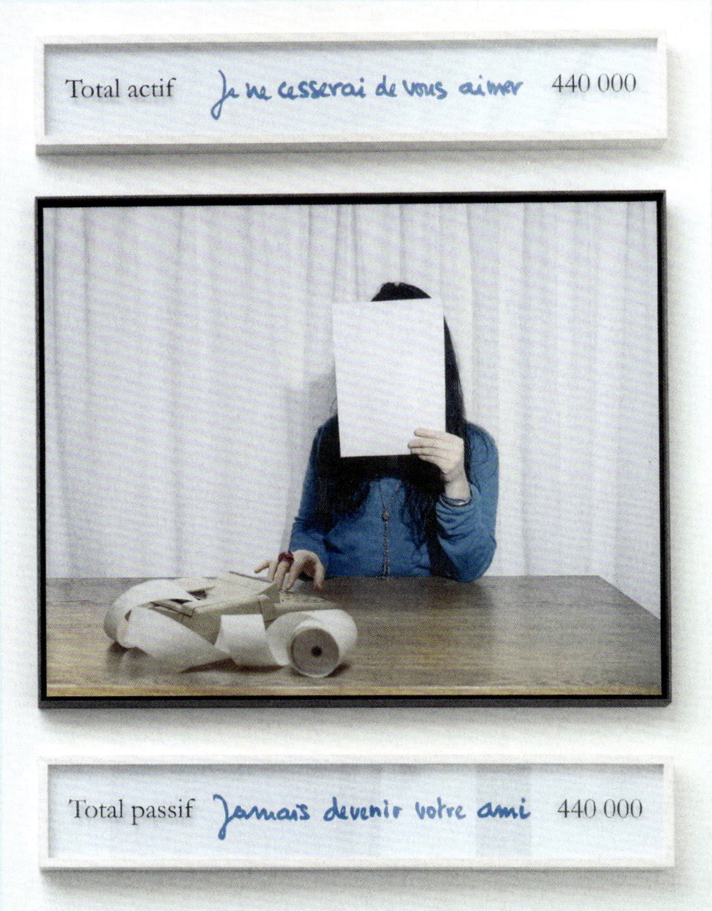

Take Care of Yourself, Sophie Calle, 2007

NARRATIVE IN COMPOSITION

USE THE FRAME AS A TOOL TO TELL A STORY

Composing minimalist photographs is an ongoing balance between simplicity and narrative; a balance between what is going to be included within the frame to help tell the story and what is deemed unnecessary and is therefore discarded. This goes beyond simply reducing the number of visual elements, though, as it also requires careful consideration about how they are going to be positioned in the frame. It is about simplifying the composition in a way that enables each element to contribute meaningfully to the overall narrative, while still maintaining the essence and feeling of minimalism.[1]

Sometimes, our images are purely documentary, so they are focused on chronicling events or scenes accurately and objectively. However, a photograph goes beyond mere representation when it tells a story with an implied or artistic interpretation that engages the viewer emotionally and prompts their imagination. Whether it's conveying a feeling, narrating a story or evoking a specific emotion, this will be a personal and subjective experience based upon individual thoughts and experiences.

Creating a minimalist image that can convey such a narrative is ultimately about how you can guide the viewer through the scene with a few key elements and still communicate a coherent visual story. Your composition will involve careful consideration, as each element can make a direct or implied suggestion. Everything in the frame has the potential to have a profound significance when it comes to the viewer's interpretation of what they are looking at, so it's all about using compositional techniques to guide the narrative: every shadow, line, colour and tone contributes to the essence and feeling of the unfolding story.

In one of many photographs taken for her project *Take Care of Yourself*, Sophie Calle creates a powerful image that captures the subject reading a letter and the suggestive emotions it can convey. We do not see much of the subject, nor the content of the letter, but this only sparks our imagination and encourages us to think about shared human experiences. This subtle suggestion ensures that the story remains open-ended, inviting personal interpretations and a connection with the audience. The title conveys an additional clue: it is a relationship break-up letter, and the project explores how different women interpret and respond to the same few words.

[1] *See* Simplicity pp. 12–3

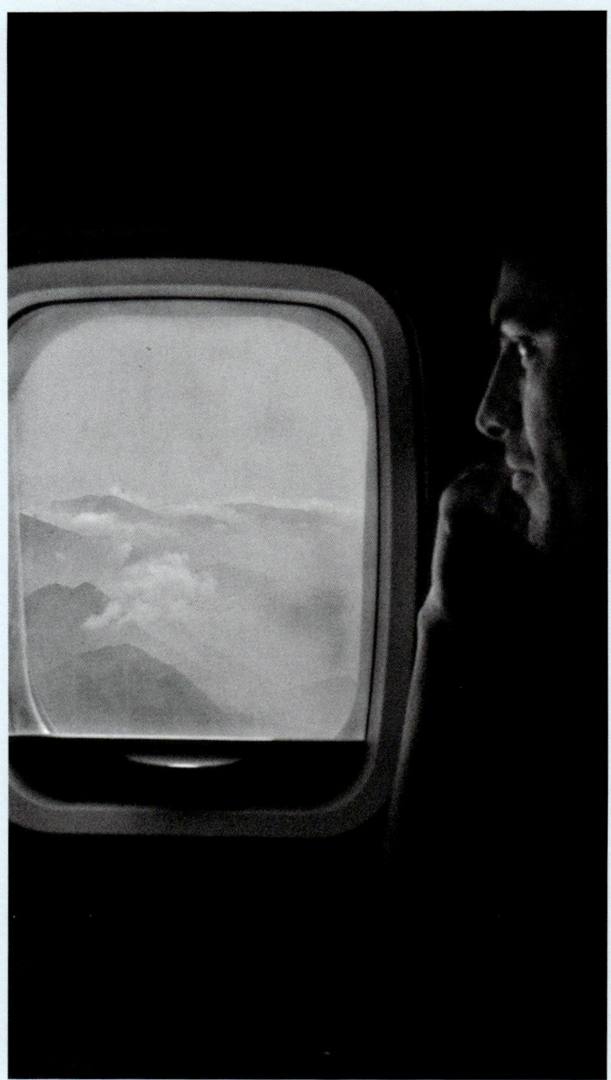

Sherpa in Flight, Jeanne Moutoussamy-Ashe, 2011

The subject and letter both take on a metaphorical role, evoking feelings of power, independence, vulnerability, resilience and hope. The narrative unfolds not just in what is shown, but in how it is captured. It is formed by the arrangement of the subject, the ambiguity and lack of visible detail revealed in their portrait. The 'flat' light and high contrast, together with large areas of negative space in the frame, simultaneously draw extra attention to the letter itself.

In *Sherpa in Flight*, Jeanne Moutoussamy-Ashe has included a few clues to help the viewer understand the story unfolding in the image. The subject is positioned looking out of an airplane window, apparently contemplating the view of the mountains below. They are clearly on a journey, although it is unclear why or where, except from the title of the image. The photographer has intimated at the story – or at least some of it – and offers just enough visual clues to guide the viewer's imagination. These subtle suggestions make the image more engaging for the audience, who must interpret the story from the limited suggestions in the composition.

The ability to suggest or imply clues in the narrative of a minimalist photograph allows for multiple interpretations, which keep the viewer engaged as they consider the various options within each image. Every person's interpretation will be subjective, and therefore at least slightly different, and will resonate with them at a personal level. The opportunity for the viewer to draw on their own experiences and project their own emotions and memories establishes a strong individual connection. As a result, a seemingly straightforward photograph can become as complicated and diverse as the people engaging with it.

CONTEXT

CREATE MEANING WITHOUT COMPLICATING THE SCENE

This image captures a seemingly simple moment of a child walking. Yet on closer inspection there are additional elements that help us uncover more of the story. A vintage car is entering the frame, slightly blurred to emphasize movement;[1] the cables and derelict building suggest an underdeveloped environment; and the building's textures[2] – and the lack of any real remaining structure – provide a rich visual backdrop that enhances the image's emotional depth. Looking closely, we can see that the scene is full of metaphors and meaning. The juxtaposition of the old, dilapidated elements, together with the young boy is significant.[3] They symbolize decay, neglect and the passage of time, compared to the boy's youth, innocence and potential.[4]

Contextualization in photography involves placing the subject within a framework that provides a background narrative or deeper understanding regarding an event, statement or idea. It is about creating a connection between the subject and their entire surroundings which will help the audience understand the broader story or setting. This can sometimes be a challenge within a minimalist composition, as this information has to be conveyed with deliberate restraint, but it is important nonetheless.

Contextual cues will add layers of meaning to a minimalist photograph, but it is not merely about showcasing the subject's surroundings. More accurately, it is about carefully considering key elements and their significance, while maintaining the minimalist ethos of simplicity and elegance. The choice of what to include to add context and what to exclude can be a delicate process.

Context is a powerful tool that can lead viewers to focus on specific aspects of the subject or its setting, which help their understanding of the scene. Establishing context in a minimalist photograph requires you to use the power of suggestion rather than overwhelming the viewer with obvious details. Aim to include just enough information to suggest what's going on, rather than revealing the whole story, as this will guide the viewer's emotional and intellectual response. The context should remain subtle and ensure that the viewer's attention is not only on the subject, but on what its presence in the given context signifies.

In contrast to more intricate compositions, minimalist photographs rely on the viewer's ability to fill in the gaps as the narrative unfolds in their imagination. There is a subtle balance between complexity and simplicity, where the image provides just enough information to spark the viewer's curiosity and prompts the audience to delve into the subtle details and forge their own unique interpretations.[5]

[1] *See* Movement pp. 88–91
[2] *See* Textures pp. 64–5
[3] *See* Juxtaposition pp. 118–9
[4] *See* Symbolism and Metaphor pp. 124–5
[5] *See* Details pp. 34–5

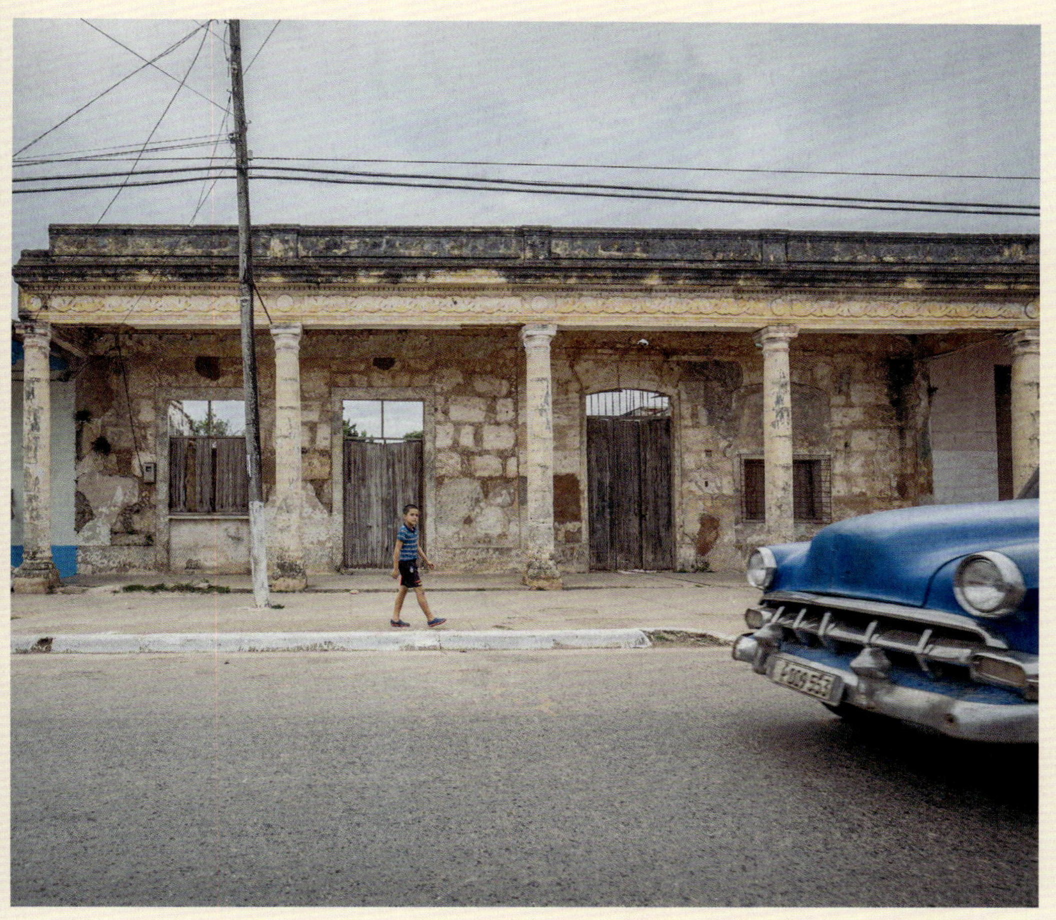

Cuban Blue, Antony Zacharias, 2018

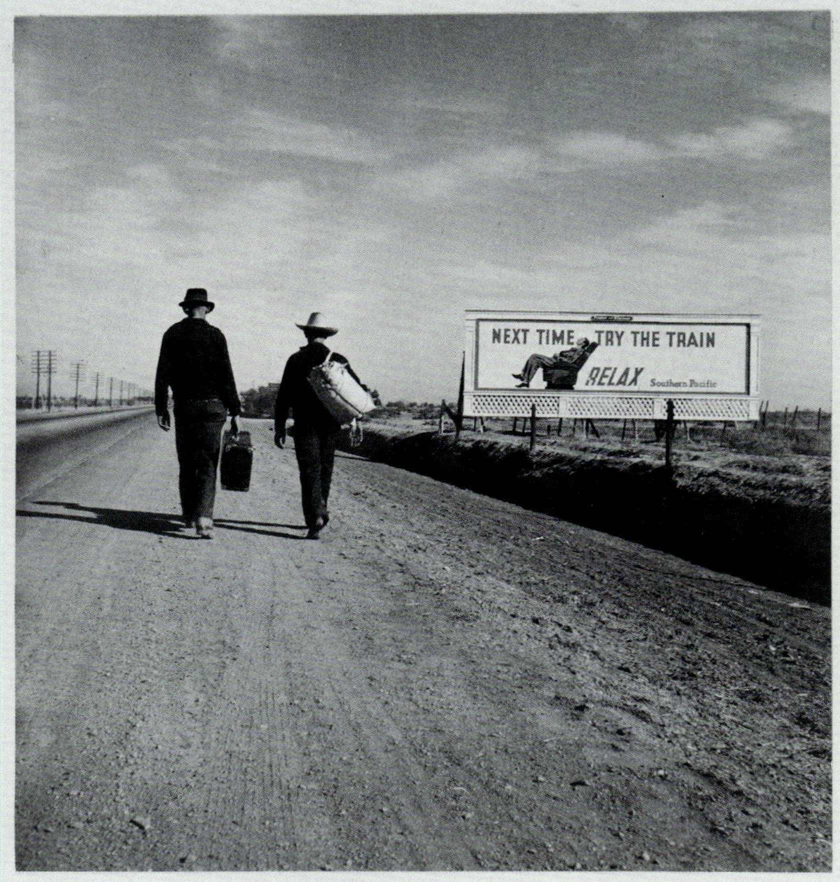

On the Road to Los Angeles, California, Dorothea Lange, 1937

ENVIRONMENTAL CLUES

CREATE A CONNECTION BETWEEN THE SUBJECT AND ITS SURROUNDINGS

The physical surroundings, conditions or setting in which a subject lives or is situated provides a unique window into their world. Careful attention to scene or setting, therefore, provides the audience with important information about the subject and their story, in addition to your motivation for creating the image.

The most striking environmental images are rooted in simplicity and avoid any clutter or overpowering elements that might distract from the core message.[1] The subject's surroundings should act as a supportive element that carefully complements the composition while hinting at additional information that can be inferred from the scene.

In particular, environmental portraits, which depict people in their natural surroundings, offer an intimate viewpoint into the subject's world. The resulting sense of connection can be powerful, infusing the image with a sense of rawness and authenticity that is both moving and compelling.

When creating an environmental portrait, consider the background elements of the image as a whole and determine how they combine to tell the subject's story, whether directly or implicitly. How do they elevate our understanding of the character, the mood and the relationships within the frame? It can, however, be challenging to achieve all of this without overwhelming the image so balance and consideration are key.

Here, Dorothea Lange has created a powerful environmental work that masterfully weaves together a sense of stark simplicity and profound depth. She has placed the elements deliberately, guiding the audience through the scene with visual suggestions that offer deeper insights into the subjects' story.

The two men are captured walking down a long, dusty and seemingly endless rural road. Next to them, an ironic sign suggests an easier, yet expensive (and likely unobtainable) mode of travel. The solitary figures in the desolate environment may stir up feelings of loneliness and introspection, or perhaps lead the viewer to think about companionship in the face of adversity. The long road may symbolize a metaphorical journey, their size in the barren landscape providing a sense of scale and revealing the enormity of the journey ahead. There is a suggestion of the resilience of human endeavour, despite environmental, and possibly economic, hardship.[2]

[1] *See* Simplicity pp. 12–3
[2] *See* Symbolism and Metaphor pp. 124–5

Unless otherwise credited, all photographs are the author's own.

16 Murray Fredericks
20 Emilie Hill
23 Harold Ross
24 Isabella Tabacchi
27 Horst P. Horst
28 Marta Bevacqua / Trunk Archive
31 © Saul Leiter Foundation
32 Richard Misrach
35 Fred Herzog
40 © The Estate of Edward Steichen / ARS, NY and DACS, London 2024
46 © Fan Ho Estate 2024, courtesy of Blue Lotus Gallery
49 Michael Kenna
50 2025 Imogen Cunningham Trust / www.ImogenCunningham.com
53 Scarlett Hooft Graafland
55 Franco Fontana
56 Photo by Lucas Zimmermann
62 David Burdeny
65 Gavin Goodman
68 Toshio Shibata
71 © Mona Kuhn '*Philipp II*, 1997'
73 Hiroshi Sugimoto
76 René Burri
85 © William Klein Estate

PICTURE CREDITS

89 Philippe Halsman / Magnum Photos
91 Copyright Alexey Titarenko, courtesy of Nailya Alexander Gallery, New York, NY
92 Andrea Torres Balaguer
95 Courtesy the artist and Tanya Bonakdar Gallery, New York / Los Angeles
96 Berenice Abbott
103 Eiji Ohashi
106 Ole Marius Joergensen
109 Courtesy Eggleston Artistic Trust and David Zwirner; Photo credit: Courtesy of Ogden Museum of Southern Art
114 © Shauneen Kelly
117 Hengki Koentjoro
118 USA, New York City, The Metropolitan Museum of Art, 1988. Image Reference ERE1988011W00006/31 (NYC3839) © Elliott Erwitt / Magnum Photos
121 Yasuhiro Ogawa
122 Robert Adams
126 Beate Sonnenberg & Johanne Mills
129 Ray Metzker
130 © Adagp, Paris, 2025; Photo: Sophie Calle, *Take Care of Yourself*, 2007, Courtesy Galerie Perrotin, Paris / Adagp image
132 Jeanne Moutoussamy-Ashe
136 Dorothea Lange / Scala Archives

ACKNOWLEDGEMENTS

This book has been a labour of love from inception and throughout. My thanks to Laura, who has helped bring this vision to life, and to Laurence King and the entire team behind the creation of this book.

To all the photographers whose work is featured, thank you – I am truly honoured to have your images in this collection. Your incredible work illuminates the essence of minimalism.

I would like to say a heartfelt thank you to my family, Shauneen and Estella for their unwavering encouragement, patience and understanding; to my daughter Thea, who is my light; my father, who is deeply loved and missed; and to Brian.

Finally, of course, my sincerest appreciation to you, my reader, for your enthusiasm and support. I hope this book inspires you to see the world through a minimalist lens and find beauty in the simplicity that abounds.